The Final Passover

A Word-Phrase Study
of the Last Days
of Jesus Christ

The Final Passover

A Word-Phrase Study
of the Last Days
of Jesus Christ

MICHAEL JAMES FITZGERALD

overduebooks

Second Edition, January 2014 (20140120)

Cover photo credit: Street in Old Jerusalem by Vladimir Blinov (Shutterstock #96795559).

ISBN-13: 978-1-887309-24-0

ISBN-10: 1-887309-24-1

Overdue Books LLC

To my wife Cristi

ACKNOWLEDGMENTS

Without my wife's support and belief in me, I don't know how, after 23 years of effort, I could have finished this book. I am also grateful for the support of my children.

I also express my thanks to Dawn Norton for reviewing the manuscript.

Most of all, I express my reverence for and my heartfelt gratitude to my Father in Heaven who inspired me to begin this study, and finally, to publish it.

CONTENTS

INTRODUCTION

This book is the result of a study I began during Easter 1986. It was then that I made my first earnest attempts to study the events in the New Testament surrounding the last days of the mortal life of Jesus Christ. I wanted to fold together the story of the Passion as told through the gospel accounts so as not to miss any of the precious details.

The gospels according to Matthew, Mark, Luke, and John each provide unique details about the events leading to Jesus's death and resurrection. My goal in this book is to: (1) identify and highlight the unique details from each of the gospels relating to the Passion, (2) to unify that material, and (3) to present my findings in a tabular format so that details could be easily distinguished.

The source for this book is the King James Version of the New Testament, with the help of Thomas M. Mumford's *Horizontal Harmony of the Four Gospels in Parallel Columns* (Salt Lake City: Deseret, 1976). No changes have been made to the original Biblical text, other than my own organizational changes.

Here are some highlights of the methods used for organizing the text.

- Most of the text provides word-for-word comparisons, where possible, but phrase-for-phrase comparisons are also made.

- Many times, words that have different meaning but have a similar function are also compared.

- If a phrase used the same or similar words but the words are transposed, most of the time, the transposition is allowed to stand.

- Where appropriate, words or phrases may be moved and placed in square brackets in order to show word or phrase comparisons.

The Passion is a story of tragedy and triumph. I have never found anything more inspiring and moving to me than the story of the last days of Jesus' mortal life. I know that Jesus was more than a man. He is the Son of God and the Savior of the world.

Though I have made every effort to avoid them, any errors or omissions in this book are solely my responsibility. But if only one reader is touched by this story, it will have been worth the effort.

PART 1

Prologue

Prologue. The Son of Man Shall Be Betrayed
Matt. 20:17–19; Mark 10:32–34; Luke 18:31–34

Matt. 20:17a And Jesus [apart in the way,] going up to Jerusalem
Mark 10:32a [And Jesus went before them:] and they were in the way going up to Jerusalem; †

Mark 10: 32b and they were amazed; and as they followed, they were afraid.

Matt. 20:17b took the twelve disciples † and said unto them,
Mark 10:32c And he took again the twelve, and began to tell them what things should happen unto him,
Luke 18:31a Then he took unto him the twelve, and said unto them,

Matt. 20:18a Behold, we go up to Jerusalem;
Mark 10:33a Behold, we go up to Jerusalem;
Luke 18:31b Saying, Behold, we go up to Jerusalem; and all things that are written by the prophets concerning the Son of man shall be accomplished.

Matt. 20:18b and the Son of man shall be betrayed unto the chief priests and unto the scribes, and they shall condemn him to death.
Mark 10:33b and the Son of man shall be delivered unto the chief priests, and unto the scribes; and they shall condemn him to death,

Matt. 20:19a And shall deliver him to the Gentiles
Mark 10:33c and shall deliver him to the Gentiles:
Luke 18:32a For he shall be delivered unto the Gentiles,

Matt. 20:19b to mock, and to scourge,
Mark 10:34a And they shall mock him, and shall scourge him, and shall spit upon him,
Luke 18:32b and shall be mocked, [and they shall scourge him,] [and spitted upon] and spitefully entreated; ‡

Matt. 20:19c and to crucify him: and the third day he shall rise again.
Mark 10:34b and shall kill him: and the third day he shall rise again.
Luke 18:33 †and put him to death: and the third day he shall rise again.

Luke 18:34 And they understood none of these things: and this saying was hid from them, neither knew they the things which were spoken.

1. An Alabaster Box of Very Precious Ointment

Matt. 26:6–12; Mark 14:3–9; John 12:1–8

Matt. 26:6	Now when Jesus was in Bethany, in the house of Simon the leper,
Mark 14:3a	And being in Bethany, in the house of Simon the leper,
John 12:1a	Then Jesus six days before the passover came to Bethany,
John 12:1b	where Lazarus was which had been dead, whom he had raised from the dead.
John 12:2	There they made him a supper: and Martha served: but Lazarus was one of them that sat at the table with him.
Matt. 26:7a	There came unto him a woman having an alabaster box of very precious ointment,
Mark 14:3b	†There came a woman having an alabaster box of [very precious]ointment of spikenard ‡; and she brake the box,
John 12:3a	Then took Mary a pound of [very costly,] ointment of spikenard, †
Matt. 26:7b	and poured it on his head, as he sat at meat.
Mark 14:3c	and poured it on his head [as he sat at meat].
John 12:3b	and anointed the feet of Jesus, and wiped his feet with her hair: and the house was filled with the odour of the ointment.
Matt. 26:8a	But when his disciples saw it, they had indignation,
Mark 14:4a	And there were some that had indignation within themselves, and
John 12:4	Then saith one of his disciples, Judas Iscariot, Simon's son, which should betray him,
Matt. 26:8b	saying, To what purpose is this waste?
Mark 14:4b	said, Why was this waste of the ointment made?
Matt. 26:9	For this ointment might have been sold for much, and given to the poor.
Mark 14:5a	For it might have been sold for more than three hundred pence, and have been given to the poor.
John 12:5	Why was not this ointment sold for three hundred pence, and given to the poor?
Mark 14:5b	And they murmured against her.
John 12:6	This he said, not that he cared for the poor; but because he was a thief, and had the bag, and bare what was put therein.
Matt. 26:10	When Jesus understood it, he said unto them, Why trouble ye the woman? for she hath wrought a good work upon me.
Mark 14:6	And Jesus said, Let her alone; why trouble ye her? she hath wrought a good work on me.
John 12:7	Then †Jesus, [said] Let her alone:

Matt. 26:11	For ye have the poor always	with you;	but me ye have not always.
Mark 14:7a	For ye have the poor [always]	with you†, and whensoever ye will ye may do them good:	but me ye have not always.
John 12:8	For [ye have] the poor always†	with you;	but me ye have not always.
Matt. 26:12a	For in that she hath	poured this ointment on	my body,
Mark 14:8a	She hath done what she could: she is come aforehand to	anoint	my body
John 12:7b	[she hath † kept this]	against the day of	my
Matt. 26:12b	she did it	for my	burial.
Mark 14:8b		to the	burying.
John 12:7c			burying†.
Mark 14:9a	Verily I say unto you, Wheresoever this gospel shall be preached throughout the whole world, this also that she hath done shall be spoken		
Mark 14:9b	of for a memorial of her.		

PART 2

The First Day of the Week

Sunday

2. Hosanna to the Son of David

Matt. 21:1–9; Mark 11:1–10; Luke 19:29–40; John 12:12–19

Matt. 21:1a	And when they drew nigh unto Jerusalem, and were come to Bethphage,
Mark 11:1a	And when they came nigh to Jerusalem, unto Bethphage and Bethany,
Luke 19:29a	And it came to pass, when he was come nigh to Bethphage and Bethany,
Matt. 21:1b	unto the mount of Olives, then sent Jesus two disciples,
Mark 11:1b	at the mount of Olives, he sendeth forth two of his disciples,
Luke 19:29b	at the mount called the mount of Olives, he sent two of his disciples,
Matt. 21:2a	Saying unto them, Go into the village over against you, and straightway
Mark 11:2a	And saith unto them, Go your way into the village over against you: and as soon as ye be entered into it,
Luke 19:30b	Saying, Go ye into the village over against you; † at your entering [in the which]
Matt. 21:2b	ye shall find an ass tied, and a colt with her: loose them, and bring them unto me.
Mark 11:2b	ye shall find a colt tied, whereon never man sat; loose him, and bring him.
Luke 19:30b	ye shall find a colt tied, whereon yet never man sat: loose him, and bring him hither.
Matt. 21:3a	And if any man say ought unto you, ye shall say, The Lord hath need of them;
Mark 11:3a	And if any man say unto you, Why do ye this? say ye that the Lord hath need of him;
Luke 19:31a	And if any man ask you, Why do ye loose him? thus shall ye say unto him, Because the Lord hath need of him.
Matt. 21:3b	and straightway he will send them.
Mark 11:3b	and straightway he will send him hither.
Matt. 21:6a	And the disciples went, and did as Jesus commanded them.
Mark 11:4a	And they went their way, and
Luke 19:32a	And they that were sent went their way, and
Mark 11:4b	found the colt tied by the door without in a place where two ways met; and they loose him.
Luke 19:32b	found even as he had said unto them.
Mark 11:5	And certain of them that stood there said unto them, What do ye, loosing the colt?
Luke 19:33	And as they were loosing the colt, the owners thereof said unto them, Why loose ye the colt?

Mark 11:6 And they said unto them even as Jesus had commanded: and they let them go.
Luke 19:34 And they said, The Lord hath need of him.

Matt. 21:7 And brought the ass, and the colt, and put on them their clothes, and set him thereon.
Mark 11:7 And they brought the colt to Jesus, and cast [on him] their garments †; and he sat upon him.
Luke 19:35 And they brought him to Jesus: and they cast [upon the colt] their garments †, and set Jesus thereon.
John 12:14a And †, when he had found a young ass, [Jesus] sat thereon;

Matt. 21:4 All this was done that it might be fulfilled which was spoken by the prophet, saying,
John 12:14b as it is written,

Matt. 21:5a Tell ye the daughter of Sion, Behold, thy King cometh unto thee,
John 12:15a Fear not, daughter of Sion: behold, thy King cometh
Zech. 9:9a Rejoice greatly, O daughter of Zion; shout, O daughter of Jerusalem: behold, thy King cometh unto thee

Matt. 21:5b and sitting upon an ass, and a colt the foal of an ass.
John 12:15b sitting on an ass's colt.
Zech. 9:9b he is just, and having salvation; lowly, and riding upon an ass, and upon a colt the foal of an ass.

John 12:16a These things understood not his disciples at the first: but when Jesus was glorified, then remembered they that these things were written of him,
John 12:16b and that they had done these things unto him.

Matt. 21:8a And a very great multitude spread their garments in the way;
Mark 11:8a And many spread their garments in the way:
Luke 19:36 And as he went, they spread their clothes in the way.

Matt. 21:8b others cut down branches from the trees, and strawed them in the way.
Mark 11:8b and others cut down branches off the trees, and strawed them in the way.

John 12:17 The people therefore that was with him when he called Lazarus out of his grave, and raised him from the dead, bare record.

John 12:18 For this cause the people also met him, for that they heard that he had done this miracle.

Luke 19:37a And when he was come nigh, even now at the descent of the mount of Olives, the whole multitude of the disciples began to rejoice and
Luke 19:37b praise God with a loud voice for all the mighty works that they had seen;

Matt. 21:9a And the multitudes that went before, and that followed, cried, saying,
Mark 11:9a And they that went before, and they that followed, cried, saying,

24

Luke 19:38a	Saying,

Matt. 21:9b	Hosanna to the Son of David: Blessed is he that cometh in the name of the Lord;
Mark 11:9b	Hosanna; Blessed is he that cometh in the name of the Lord:
Luke 19:38b	Blessed be the King that cometh in the name of the Lord:

Matt. 21:9c	Hosanna in the highest.
Mark 11:9	Hosanna in the highest.
Luke 19:38c	peace in heaven, and glory in the highest.

Mark 11:10 — Blessed be the kingdom of our father David, that cometh in the name of the Lord:

Luke 19:39	And some of the Pharisees from among the multitude said unto him, Master, rebuke thy disciples.
Luke 19:40	And he answered and said unto them, I tell you that, if these should hold their peace, the stones would immediately cry out.
John 12:19	The Pharisees therefore said among themselves, Perceive ye how ye prevail nothing? behold, the world is gone after him.

3. He Beheld the City and Wept

Matt. 21:10–11. 17; Mark 11:11; Luke 19:41–44

Luke 19:41	¶ And when he was come near, he beheld the city, and wept over it,
Luke 19:42	Saying, If thou hadst known, even thou, at least in this thy day, the things which belong unto thy peace! but now they are hid from thine eyes.
Luke 19:43	For the days shall come upon thee, that thine enemies shall cast a trench about thee, and compass thee round, and keep thee in on every side,
Luke 19:44a	And shall lay thee even with the ground, and thy children within thee; and they shall not leave in thee one stone upon another;
Luke 19:44b	because thou knewest not the time of thy visitation.
Matt. 21:10	And when he was come into Jerusalem, all the city was moved, saying, Who is this?
Matt. 21:11	And the multitude said, This is Jesus the prophet of Nazareth of Galilee.
Mark 11:11a	And Jesus entered into Jerusalem, and into the temple: and when he had looked round about upon all things, and now the eventide was come,
Matt. 21:17	¶ And he left them, and went out of the city into Bethany; and he lodged there.
Mark 11:11b	he went out unto Bethany with the twelve.

PART 3

The Second Day of the Week

Monday

4. Let Not Fruit Grow on Thee
Matt. 21:18–19; Mark 12:12–14

Matt. 21:18   Now in the morning as he returned into the city, he hungered.
Mark 11:12   ¶ And on the morrow, when they were come from Bethany, he was hungry:

Matt. 21:19a   And when he saw a fig tree in the way, he came to it,
Mark 11:13a   And seeing a fig tree afar off having leaves, he came, if haply he might find any thing thereon:

Matt. 21:19b   and found nothing thereon, but leaves only,
Mark 11:13b   and when he came to it, he found nothing but leaves; for the time of figs was not yet.

Matt. 21:19c   and said unto it, Let no fruit grow on thee henceforward for ever.
Mark 11:14   And Jesus answered and said unto it, No man eat fruit of thee hereafter for ever. And his disciples heard it.

Matt. 21:19d   And presently the fig tree withered away.

5. Ye Have Made It a Den of Thieves
Matt. 21:12–13; Mark 11:15–17; Luke 19:45–46

Matt. 21:12a   ¶ And Jesus went into the temple of God,
Mark 11:15a   And they come to Jerusalem: and Jesus went into the temple,
Luke 19:45a   And he went into the temple,

Matt. 21:12b   and cast out all them that sold and bought in the temple,
Mark 11:15b   and began to cast out them that sold and bought in the temple,
Luke 19:45b   and began to cast out them that sold therein, and them that bought;

Matt. 21:12c   and overthrew the tables of the moneychangers, and the seats of them that sold doves,
Mark 11:15c   and overthrew the tables of the moneychangers, and the seats of them that sold doves;

Mark 11:16   And would not suffer that any man should carry any vessel through the temple.

Matt. 21:13a   And said unto them, It is written, My house shall be called the house of prayer;
Mark 11:17a   And he taught, saying unto them, Is it not written, My house shall be called of all nations the house of prayer?

Luke 19:46a	Saying unto them, It is written, My house is the house of prayer:
Matt. 21:13b	but ye have made it a den of thieves.
Mark 11:17b	but ye have made it a den of thieves.
Luke 19:46b	but ye have made it a den of thieves.

6. Out of the Mouths of Babes

Matt. 21:14–16; Mark 11:18; Luke 19:47–48

Matt. 21:14	And the blind and the lame came to him in the temple; and he healed them.
Matt. 21:15a	And when the chief priests and scribes saw the wonderful things that he did, and the children crying in the temple,
Matt. 21:15b	and saying, Hosanna to the Son of David; they were sore displeased,
Matt. 21:16a	And said unto him, Hearest thou what these say? And Jesus saith unto them, Yea; have ye never read,
Matt. 21:16b	Out of the mouth of babes and sucklings thou hast perfected praise?
Mark 11:18a	And the scribes and chief priests
Luke 19:47a	And he taught daily in the temple. But the[2x] [scribes] [and] the chief priests ‡† and the chief of the people heard it,
Mark 11:18b	sought how they might destroy him: for they feared him,
Luke 19:47b	sought to destroy him,
Mark 11:18c	because all the people was astonished at his doctrine.
Luke 19:48	And could not find what they might do: for all the people were very attentive to hear him.

PART 4

The Third Day of the Week

Tuesday

7. The Fig Tree Withered Away
Matt. 21:20–22; Mark 11:20–26

Mark 11:20 ¶ And in the morning, as they passed by, they saw the fig tree dried up from the roots.

Matt. 21:20a And when the disciples saw it, they marvelled, saying,
Mark 11:21a And Peter calling to remembrance saith unto him,

Matt. 21:20b How soon is the fig tree withered away!
Mark 11:21b Master, behold, the fig tree which thou cursedst is withered away.

Matt. 21:21a Jesus answered and said unto them, Verily I say unto you, If ye have faith, and doubt not,
Mark 11:22 And Jesus answering saith unto them, Have faith in God.

Matt. 21:21b For verily I say unto you, ye shall not only do this which is done to the fig tree, but also if ye shall say unto this mountain,
Mark 11:23a That whosoever shall say unto this mountain,

Matt. 21:21c Be thou removed, and be thou cast into the sea;
Mark 11:23b Be thou removed, and be thou cast into the sea; and shall not doubt in his heart, but shall believe that those things which he saith shall come to pass;

Matt. 21:21d it shall be done.
Mark 11:23c he shall have whatsoever he saith.

Matt. 21:22 Therefore I say unto you, And all things, whatsoever ye shall ask in prayer, believing, ye shall receive.
Mark 11:24a What things soever ye desire, when ye pray, believe that ye receive them, receive them,

Mark 11:24b and ye shall have them.

Mark 11:25 And when ye stand praying, forgive, if ye have ought against any: that your Father also which is in heaven may forgive you your trespasses.

Mark 11:26 But if ye do not forgive, neither will your Father which is in heaven forgive your trespasses.

8. Who Gave Thee This Authority?

Matt. 21:23–27; Mark 11:27–33; Luke 20:1–8

Matt. 21:23a	¶ And when he was come into the temple, † as he was teaching,
Mark 11:27a	¶ And they come again to Jerusalem: [in the temple,] and as he was walking, †
Luke 20:1a	And it came to pass, that on one of those days, [in the temple,] as he taught the people †
Matt. 21:23b	[the chief priests † came unto him [and the elders of the people]]
Mark 11:27b	† the chief priests, and the scribes, and the elders, [there come to him]
Luke 20:1b	and preached the gospel, the chief priests came upon him with the elders,
Matt. 21:23c	and said, By what authority doest thou these things? and who gave thee this authority?
Mark 11:28a	And say unto him, By what authority doest thou these things? and who gave thee this authority
Luke 20:2	And spake unto him, saying, Tell us, by what authority doest thou these things? or who is he that gave thee this authority?
Mark 11:28b	to do these things?
Matt. 21:24a	And Jesus answered and said unto them, I also will ask you one thing, which if ye tell me,
Mark 11:29a	And Jesus answered and said unto them, I will also ask of you one question, and answer me,
Luke 20:3	And he answered and said unto them, I will also ask you one thing; and answer me:
Matt. 21:24b	I in like wise will tell you by what authority I do these things.
Mark 11:29b	and I will tell you by what authority I do these things.
Matt. 21:25a	The baptism of John, whence was it? from heaven, or of men?
Mark 11:30	The baptism of John, was it from heaven, or of men? answer me.
Luke 20:4	The baptism of John, was it from heaven, or of men?
Matt. 21:25b	And they reasoned with themselves, saying, If we shall say, From heaven; he will say unto us, Why did ye not then believe him?
Mark 11:31	And they reasoned with themselves, saying, If we shall say, From heaven; he will say, Why then did ye not believe him?
Luke 20:5	And they reasoned with themselves, saying, If we shall say, From heaven; he will say, Why then believed ye him not?
Matt. 21:26a	But if we shall say, Of men; we fear the people;
Mark 11:32a	But if we shall say, Of men; they feared the people:
Luke 20:6a	But and if we say, Of men; all the people will stone us:

34

Matt. 21:26b	for all	hold	John as	a prophet.
Mark 11:32b	for all men	counted	John, that he	was a prophet indeed.
Luke 20:6b	for they	be persuaded that John		was a prophet.

Matt. 21:27a	And they answered [and said,]	Jesus, †	We cannot	tell.
Mark 11:33a	And they answered and said	unto Jesus,	We cannot	tell.
Luke 20:7	And they answered,	that	they could not	tell whence it was.

Matt. 21:27b	And he	said unto them,	Neither	tell I you by what authority I do these things.
Mark 11:33b	And Jesus answering	saith unto them,	Neither do	I tell you by what authority I do these things.
Luke 20:8	And Jesus	said unto them,	Neither	tell I you by what authority I do these things.

9. A Certain Man Had Two Sons
Matt. 21:28–32

Matt. 21:28 ¶ But what think ye? A certain man had two sons; and he came to the first, and said, Son, go work to day in my vineyard.

Matt. 21:29 He answered and said, I will not: but afterward he repented, and went.

Matt. 21:30 And he came to the second, and said likewise. And he answered and said, I go, sir: and went not.

Matt. 21:31a Whether of them twain did the will of his father? They say unto him, The first. Jesus saith unto them, Verily I say unto you, That the publicans

Matt. 21:31b and the harlots go into the kingdom of God before you.

Matt. 21:32a For John came unto you in the way of righteousness, and ye believed him not: but the publicans and the harlots believed him: and ye,

Matt. 21:32b when ye had seen it, repented not afterward, that ye might believe him.

10. A Certain Man Planted a Vineyard
Matt. 21:33–41; Mark 12:1–9; Luke 20:9–16

Matt. 21:33a	¶	Hear	another parable: There was	a certain	householder, which	planted a vineyard,
Mark 12:1a	And	he began to speak unto	them	by	parables.	A certain man	planted a vineyard,
Luke 20:9a	Then	began he to speak to	the people	this	parable;	A certain man	planted a vineyard,

| Matt. 21:33b | and | hedged it | round | about, | and digged a | winepress in it, | and built a tower, |
| Mark 12:1b | and set an | hedge | [it] | about†, | and digged a place for the | winefat, | and built a tower, |

35

Matt. 21:33c — and let it out to husbandmen, and went into a far country:
Mark 12:1c — and let it out to husbandmen, and went into a far country.
Luke 20:9b — and let it forth to husbandmen, and went into a far country for a long time.

Matt. 21:34a — And when the time of the fruit drew near, he sent his servants to the husbandmen,
Mark 12:2a — And at the season he sent † a servant [to the husbandmen],
Luke 20:10a — And at the season he sent a servant to the husbandmen,

Matt. 21:34b — that they might receive the fruits of it.
Mark 12:2b — that he might receive from the husbandmen of the fruit of the vineyard.
Luke 20:10b — that they should give him of the fruit of the vineyard:

Matt. 21:35 — And the husbandmen took his servants, and beat one, and killed another, and stoned another.
Mark 12:3 — And they caught him, and beat him, and sent him away empty.
Luke 20:10c — but the husbandmen beat him, and sent him away empty.

Matt. 21:36a — Again, he sent other servants more than the first:
Mark 12:4a — And again he sent unto them another servant;
Luke 20:11a — And again he sent another servant:

Matt. 21:36b — and they did unto them likewise.
Mark 12:4b — and at him they cast stones, and wounded him in the head,
Luke 20:11b — and they beat him also,

Mark 12:4c — and † [handled] shamefully ‡ [sent him away].
Luke 20:11c — and entreated him shamefully, and sent him away empty.

Mark 12:5 — And again he sent another; and him they killed, and many others; beating some, and killing some.

Matt. 21:37a — But last of all
Mark 12:6a — Having yet therefore one son, his wellbeloved,
Luke 20:13a — Then said the lord of the vineyard, What shall I do?

Matt. 21:37b — he sent unto them his son, saying, They will reverence my son.
Mark 12:6b — he sent † also last unto them [him], [my ‡ son] saying, They will reverence my son.
Luke 20:13b — I will send ‡: [beloved] it may be they will reverence him when they see him.

Matt. 21:38a	But when the husbandmen saw the son, they said among themselves,
Mark 12:7a	But those husbandmen said among themselves,
Luke 20:14a	But when the husbandmen saw him, they reasoned among themselves, saying,
Matt. 21:38b	This is the heir; come, let us kill him, and let us seize on his inheritance.
Mark 12:7b	This is the heir; come, let us kill him, and the inheritance shall be ours.
Luke 20:14b	This is the heir: come, let us kill him, that the inheritance may be ours.
Matt. 21:39	And they caught him, and cast him out of the vineyard, and slew him.
Mark 12:8	And they took him, [and cast him out of the vineyard,] and killed him, †
Luke 20:15a	So they cast him out of the vineyard, and killed him.
Matt. 21:40	When [therefore] the lord † of the vineyard † cometh, what will he do unto those husbandmen?
Mark 12:9a	What shall therefore the lord of the vineyard do?
Luke 20:15b	What † shall [therefore] the lord of the vineyard do unto them?
Matt. 21:41a	They say unto him, He will miserably destroy those wicked men,
Mark 12:9b	he will come and destroy the husbandmen,
Luke 20:16a	He shall come and destroy these husbandmen,
Matt. 21:41b	and will let out his vineyard unto other husbandmen, which shall render him the fruits in their seasons.
Mark 12:9c	and will give the vineyard unto others.
Luke 20:16b	and shall give the vineyard to others.
Luke 20:16c	And when they heard it, they said, God forbid.

11. The Stone Which the Builders Rejected

Matt. 21:42–46; Mark 12:10–12; Luke 20:17–19

Matt. 21:42a	And Jesus saith unto them, Did ye never read in the scriptures,
Mark 12:10a	And have ye not read this scripture;
Luke 20:17a	And he beheld them, and said, What is this then that is written,
Matt. 21:42b	The stone which the builders rejected, the same is become the head of the corner:
Mark 12:10b	The stone which the builders rejected is become the head of the corner:
Luke 20:17b	The stone which the builders rejected, the same is become the head of the corner?
Psalms 118:22	The stone which the builders refused is become the head stone of the corner.

37

Matt. 21:42c	this	is	the Lord's doing, and	it is marvellous in our eyes?	
Mark 12:11	This	was	the Lord's doing, and	it is marvellous in our eyes?	
Psalms 118:23	This	is	the Lord's doing;	it is marvellous in our eyes.	

Matt. 21:43 Therefore say I unto you, The kingdom of God shall be taken from you, and given to a nation bringing forth the fruits thereof.

Matt. 21:44	And	whosoever	shall fall on	this stone shall be broken: but on whomsoever it shall fall, it will grind him to powder.
Luke 20:18		Whosoever	shall fall upon that	stone shall be broken; but on whomsoever it shall fall, it will grind him to powder.

Matt. 21:45a	And	when the chief priests and Pharisees	had heard his parables,	they perceived
Mark 12:12b	for			they knew
Luke 20:19a	¶ And	the chief priests	and the scribes	
Luke 20:19c	for			they perceived

Matt. 21:45b	that he	spake	of them.
Mark 12:12c	that he had	spoken the parable	against them:
Luke 20:19d	that he had	spoken this parable	against them.

Matt. 21:46a	But	when they	sought to lay hands	on him,	they feared the multitude,
Mark 12:12a	And	they	sought to lay hold	on him, but	feared the people:
Luke 20:19b		the same hour	sought to lay hands	on him; and	they feared the people:

Matt. 21:46b	because they took him for a prophet.
Mark 12:12c	and they left him, and went their way.

12. A King Made a Marriage for His Son
Matthew 22:1–14

Matt. 22:1 And Jesus answered and spake unto them again by parables, and said,

Matt. 22:2 The kingdom of heaven is like unto a certain king, which made a marriage for his son,

Matt. 22:3 And sent forth his servants to call them that were bidden to the wedding: and they would not come.

Matt. 22:4a Again, he sent forth other servants, saying, Tell them which are bidden, Behold, I have prepared my dinner: my oxen and my fatlings

Matt. 22:4b are killed, and all things are ready: come unto the marriage.

Matt. 22:5	But they made light of it, and went their ways, one to his farm, another to his merchandise:
Matt. 22:6	And the remnant took his servants, and entreated them spitefully, and slew them.
Matt. 22:7	But when the king heard thereof, he was wroth: and he sent forth his armies, and destroyed those murderers, and burned up their city.
Matt. 22:8	Then saith he to his servants, The wedding is ready, but they which were bidden were not worthy.
Matt. 22:9	Go ye therefore into the highways, and as many as ye shall find, bid to the marriage.
Matt. 22:10a / Matt. 22:10b	So those servants went out into the highways, and gathered together all as many as they found, both bad and good: and the wedding was furnished with guests.
Matt. 22:11	¶ And when the king came in to see the guests, he saw there a man which had not on a wedding garment:
Matt. 22:12	And he saith unto him, Friend, how camest thou in hither not having a wedding garment? And he was speechless.
Matt. 22:13a / Matt. 22:13b	Then said the king to the servants, Bind him hand and foot, and take him away, and cast him into outer darkness; there shall be weeping and gnashing of teeth.
Matt. 22:14	For many are called, but few are chosen.

13. Render Therefore unto Caesar

Matt. 22:15–22; Mark 12:13–17; Luke 20:20–26

Matt. 22:15a	¶ Then			went		the	Pharisees,
Mark 12:13a	¶ And		they	send	unto him certain of	the	Pharisees and of the Herodians,
Luke 20:20a	And	they watched him, and		sent forth			spies,
Matt. 22:16a	And		they	sent out	unto him		their disciples with the Herodians,
Matt. 22:15b					and took counsel	how	they might entangle him in his talk.
Mark 12:13b						to	catch him in his words.
Luke 20:20b	which should feign themselves just men,					that	they might take hold of his words,
Luke 20:20c	that so they might deliver him unto the power and authority of the governor.						

Matt. 22:16b	saying, Master, we know that thou art true, and teachest the way of God in truth,
Mark 12:14a	And when they were come, they say unto him, Master, we know that thou art true, but teachest the way of God in truth:
Luke 20:21a	And they asked him, saying, Master, we know that thou sayest and teachest rightly,
Luke 20:21c	but teachest the way of God truly:
Matt. 22:16c	neither carest thou for any man: for thou regardest not the person of men.
Mark 12:14b	and carest for no man: for thou regardest not the person of men,
Luke 20:21b	neither acceptest thou the person of any,
Matt. 22:17	Tell us therefore, What thinkest thou? Is it lawful to give tribute unto Caesar, or not?
Mark 12:14d	Is it lawful to give tribute to Caesar, or not?
Luke 20:22	Is it lawful for us to give tribute unto Caesar, or no?
Mark 12:15a	Shall we give, or shall we not give?
Matt. 22:18	But Jesus perceived their wickedness, and said, Why tempt ye me, ye hypocrites?
Mark 12:15b	But he, knowing their hypocrisy, said unto them, Why tempt ye me?
Luke 20:23	But he perceived their craftiness, and said unto them, Why tempt ye me?
Matt. 22:19a	Shew me the tribute money.
Mark 12:15c	bring me a penny, that I may see it.
Luke 20:24a	Shew me a penny.
Matt. 22:19b	And they brought unto him a penny.
Mark 12:16a	And they brought it.
Matt. 22:20	And he saith unto them, Whose is this image and superscription?
Mark 12:16b	And he saith unto them, Whose is this image and superscription?
Luke 20:24b	Whose image and superscription hath it?
Matt. 22:21a	They say unto him, Caesar's.
Mark 12:16c	And they said unto him, Caesar's.
Luke 20:24c	They answered and said, Caesar's.
Matt. 22:21b	Then [he] saith † unto them, Render therefore unto Caesar the things which are Caesar's;
Mark 12:17a	And Jesus answering said unto them, Render unto Caesar the things that are Caesar's,
Luke 20:25a	And he said unto them, Render therefore unto Caesar the things which be Caesar's,

Matt. 22:21c	and unto	God the things that	are God's.						
Mark 12:17b	and to	God the things that	are God's.						
Luke 20:25b	and unto	God the things which	be God's.						

Matt. 22:22a	When they had heard these words,	they marvelled,
Mark 12:17c	And	they marvelled at him.
Luke 20:26a	And they could not take hold of his words before the people: and	they marvelled at his answer,

Matt. 22:2b	and left him, and went their way.
Luke 20:26b	and held their peace.

14. Whose Wife Shall She Be?

Matt. 22:23–33; Mark 12:18–27; Luke 20:27–39

Matt. 22:23	¶ The same day	came to	him	the Sadducees, which say	that	there is no resurrection,	and	asked him,
Mark 12:18	¶ Then	come unto	him	the Sadducees, which say		there is no resurrection;	and they	asked him, saying,
Luke 20:27	¶ Then	came to	him certain of	the Sadducees, which deny that		there is any resurrection;	and they	asked him,

Matt. 22:24a	Saying, Master, Moses said,	If a	man [his	brother] die, † ‡ shall marry	his	wife,
Mark 12:19a	Master, Moses wrote unto us,	If a	man's	brother die,	and leave his	wife behind him,
Luke 20:28a	Saying, Master, Moses wrote unto us,	If any	man's	brother die,	having a	wife,

Matt. 22:24b	[having	no	children,]
Mark 12:19b	and leave	no	children,
Luke 20:28b	and he die	without	children,

Matt. 22:24c	his brother shall	marry	his wife, and raise up seed unto his brother.
Mark 12:19b	that his brother should	take	his wife, and raise up seed unto his brother.
Luke 20:28c	that his brother should	take	his wife, and raise up seed unto his brother.

Matt. 22:25a	Now	there were	with us	seven brethren:
Mark 12:20a	Now	there were		seven brethren:
Luke 20:29a		There were therefore		seven brethren:

Matt. 22:25b	and the first, when he had married	a wife,	deceased, and, having	no	issue,
Mark 12:20b	and the first	took	a wife, and	dying	left	no seed.
Luke 20:29b	and the first	took	a wife, and	died		without children.

Matt. 22:26a	Likewise the second also,
Mark 12:21a	And the second took her, and died, neither left he any seed:
Luke 20:30	And the second took her to wife, and he died childless.
Matt. 22:26b	and the third,
Mark 12:21b	and the third likewise.
Luke 20:31a	And the third took her;
Matt. 22:26c	unto the seventh.
Mark 12:22a	And the seven had her, and left no seed:
Luke 20:31b	and in like manner the seven also: and they left no children, and died.
Matt. 22:27	And last of all the woman died also.
Mark 12:22b	last of all the woman died also.
Luke 20:32	Last of all the woman died also.
Matt. 22:28	Therefore in the resurrection whose wife shall she be of the seven? for they all had her.
Mark 12:23	In the resurrection therefore, when they shall rise, whose wife shall she be of them? for the seven had her to wife.
Luke 20:33	Therefore in the resurrection whose wife of them is she? for seven had her to wife.
Matt. 22:29	Jesus answered and said unto them, Ye do err, not knowing the scriptures, nor the power of God.
Mark 12:24	And Jesus answering said unto them, Do ye not therefore err, because ye know not the scriptures, neither the power of God?
Luke 20:34a	And Jesus answering said unto them,
Luke 20:34b	The children of this world marry, and are given in marriage:
Luke 20:35a	But they which shall be accounted worthy to obtain that world,
Matt. 22:30a	For in the resurrection they neither marry, nor are given in marriage,
Mark 12:25a	For when they shall rise from the dead, they neither marry, nor are given in marriage;
Luke 20:35b	and the resurrection from the dead, neither marry, nor are given in marriage:
Matt. 22:30b	but are as the angels of God in heaven.
Mark 12:25b	but are as the angels which are in heaven.
Luke 20:36a	Neither can they die any more: for they are equal unto the angels;
Luke 20:36b	and are the children of God, being the children of the resurrection.

Matt. 22:31a But as touching the resurrection of the dead,
Mark 12:26a And as touching the dead, that they rise:
Luke 20:37a Now that the dead are raised,

Matt. 22:31b have ye not read that which was spoken unto you by God, saying,
Mark 12:26b have ye not read in the book of Moses, how in the bush God spake unto him, saying,
Luke 20:37b Moses shewed at the bush,

Matt. 22:32a I am the God of Abraham, and the God of Isaac, and the God of Jacob?
Mark 12:26c I am the God of Abraham, and the God of Isaac, and the God of Jacob?
Luke 20:37c when he calleth the Lord the God of Abraham, and the God of Isaac, and the God of Jacob.

Matt. 22:32b God is not the God of the dead, but of the living.
Mark 12:27 He is not the God of the dead, but the God of the living; ye therefore do greatly err.
Luke 20:38 For he is not a God of the dead, but of the living; for all live unto him.

Matt. 22:33 And when the multitude heard this, they were astonished at his doctrine.

Luke 20:39 ¶ Then certain of the scribes answering said, Master, thou hast well said.

15. Thou Shalt Love the Lord thy God
Matt. 22:34–40; Mark 12:28–34; Luke 20:40

Matt. 22:34 ¶ But when the Pharisees had heard that he had put the Sadducees to silence, they were gathered together.

Matt. 22:35a Then one of them, which was a lawyer,
Mark 12:28a ¶ And one of the scribes came, and having heard them reasoning together, and perceiving that he had answered them well,

Matt. 22:35b asked him a question, tempting him, and saying,
Mark 12:28b asked him,

Matt. 22:36 Master, which is the great commandment in the law?
Mark 12:28c Which is the first commandment of all?

Matt. 22:37a Jesus said unto him,
Mark 12:29 And Jesus answered him, The first of all the commandments is, Hear, O Israel; The Lord our God is one Lord:

| Matt. 22:37b | Thou shalt love the Lord thy God with all thy heart, and with all thy soul, and with all thy mind. |
| Mark 12:30a | And thou shalt love the Lord thy God with all thy heart, and with all thy soul, and with all thy mind, and with all thy strength: |

| Matt. 22:38 | This is the first and great commandment. |
| Mark 12:30b | this is the first commandment. |

| Matt. 22:39 | And the second is like unto it, Thou shalt love thy neighbor as thyself. |
| Mark 12:31 | And the second is like, namely this, Thou shalt love thy neighbor as thyself. There is none other commandment greater than these. |

| Luke 22:40 | On these two commandments hang all the law and the prophets. |

| Mark 12:32 | And the scribe said unto him, Well, Master, thou hast said the truth: for there is one God; and there is none other but he: |

| Mark 12:33a | And to love him with all the heart, and with all the understanding, and with all the soul, and with all the strength, |

| Mark 12:33b | and to love his neighbour as himself, is more than all whole burnt offerings and sacrifices. |

| Mark 12:34a | And when Jesus saw that he answered discreetly, he said unto him, Thou art not far from the kingdom of God. |

16. What Think Ye of Christ?

Matt. 22:41–46; Mark 12:35–37; Luke 20:41–44

| Matt. 22:41a | ¶ While the Pharisees were gathered together, |

Matt. 22:41b	Jesus asked them,
Mark 12:35a	¶ And Jesus answered and said, while he taught in the temple,
Luke 20:41a	And he said unto them,

| Matt. 22:42a | Saying, What think ye of Christ? whose son is he? |

| Matt. 22:42b | They say unto him, The Son of David. |

| Mark 12:36b | How say the scribes that Christ is the Son of David? |
| Luke 20:41b | How say they that Christ is David's son? |

| Matt. 22:43 | He saith unto them, How then doth David in spirit call him Lord, saying, |

44

Mark 12:36a	For David himself said by the Holy Ghost, in the book of Psalms,
Luke 20:42a	And David himself saith in the book of Psalms,
Matt. 22:44	The Lord said unto my Lord, Sit thou on my right hand, till I make thine enemies thy footstool?
Mark 12:36b	The Lord said to my Lord, Sit thou on my right hand, till I make thine enemies thy footstool.
Luke 20:42	The Lord said unto my Lord, Sit thou on my right hand,
Luke 20:43	Till I make thine enemies thy footstool.
Matt. 22:45	If David then call him Lord, how is he his son?
Mark 12:37a	David therefore himself calleth him Lord; and whence is he then his son?
Luke 22:44	David therefore calleth him Lord, how is he then his son?
Mark 12:37b	An the common people heard him gladly.
Matt. 22:46	And no man was able to answer him a word, neither durst any man from that day forth ask him any more questions.
Mark 12:34b	And [after that] no man † durst ask him any question.
Luke 20:40	And after that they durst not ask him any question at all.

17. Wo Unto You

Matt. 23:1–39; Mark 12:38–40; Luke 20:45–47

Matt. 23:1	Then spake Jesus to the multitude, and to his disciples,
Mark 12:38a	¶ And he said them in his doctrine,
Luke 20:45	¶ Then [he said] in the audience of all the people † unto his disciples,
Matt. 23:2	Saying, The scribes and the Pharisees sit in Moses' seat:
Mark 12:38b	Beware of the scribes,
Luke 29:46a	Beware of the scribes,
Matt. 23:3	All therefore whatsoever they bid you observe, that observe and do; but do not ye after their works: for they say, and do not.
Matt. 23:4a	For they bind heavy burdens and grievous to be borne, and lay them on men's shoulders;
Matt. 23:4b	but they themselves will not move them with one of their fingers.
Matt. 23:5a	But all their works they do for to be seen of men: they make broad their phylacteries,
Matt. 23:5b	and enlarge the borders of their garments,

Mark 12:38c	which love to go in long clothing,
Luke 20:46b	which desire to walk in long robes,
Matt. 23:6	And love the uppermost rooms at feasts, and the chief seats in the synagogues,
Mark 12:39	And [the uppermost rooms at feasts;] and † the chief seats in the synagogues,
Luke 20:46d	and [the chief rooms at feasts;] and † the highest seats in the synagogues,
Matt. 23:7	And greetings in the markets, and to be called of men, Rabbi, Rabbi.
Mark 12:38c	and love salutations in the marketplaces,
Luke 20:46c	and love greetings in the markets,
Matt. 23:8	But be not ye called Rabbi: for one is your Master, even Christ; and all ye are brethren.
Matt. 23:9	And call no man your father upon the earth: for one is your Father, which is in heaven.
Matt. 23:10	Neither be ye called masters: for one is your Master, even Christ.
Matt. 23:11	But he that is greatest among you shall be your servant.
Matt. 23:12	And whosoever shall exalt himself shall be abased; and he that shall humble himself shall be exalted.
Matt. 23:13a	¶ But woe unto you, scribes and Pharisees, hypocrites! for ye shut up the kingdom of heaven against men:
Matt. 23:13b	for ye neither go in yourselves, neither suffer ye them that are entering to go in.
Matt. 23:14a	Woe unto you, scribes and Pharisees, hypocrites! for ye devour widows' houses,
Mark 12:40a	Which devour widows' houses,
Luke 20:47a	Which devour widows' houses,
Matt. 23:14b	and for a pretence make long prayer: therefore ye shall receive the greater damnation.
Mark 12:40b	and for a pretence make long prayers: these shall receive greater damnation.
Luke 20:47b	and for a shew make long prayers: the same shall receive greater damnation.
Matt. 23:15a	Woe unto you, scribes and Pharisees, hypocrites! for ye compass sea and land to make one proselyte,
Matt. 23:15b	and when he is made, ye make him twofold more the child of hell than yourselves.
Matt. 23:16a	Woe unto you, ye blind guides, which say, Whosoever shall swear by the temple, it is nothing;
Matt. 23:16b	but whosoever shall swear by the gold of the temple, he is a debtor!

Matt. 23:17	Ye fools and blind: for whether is greater, the gold, or the temple that sanctifieth the gold?
Matt. 23:18	And, Whosoever shall swear by the altar, it is nothing; but whosoever sweareth by the gift that is upon it, he is guilty.
Matt. 23:19	Ye fools and blind: for whether is greater, the gift, or the altar that sanctifieth the gift?
Matt. 23:20	Whoso therefore shall swear by the altar, sweareth by it, and by all things thereon.
Matt. 23:21	And whoso shall swear by the temple, sweareth by it, and by him that dwelleth therein.
Matt. 23:22	And he that shall swear by heaven, sweareth by the throne of God, and by him that sitteth thereon.
Matt. 23:23a **Luke 11:42a**	Woe unto you, scribes and Pharisees, hypocrites! for ye pay tithe of mint and anise and cummin, But woe unto you, Pharisees! for ye tithe mint and rue and all manner of herbs,
Matt. 23:23b **Luke 11:42b**	and have omitted the weightier matters of the law, judgment, mercy, and faith: and pass over judgment and the love of God:
Matt. 23:23c **Luke 11:42c**	these ought ye to have done, and not to leave the other undone. these ought ye to have done, and not to leave the other undone.
Matt. 23:24	Ye blind guides, which strain at a gnat, and swallow a camel.
Matt. 23:25a **Matt. 23:25b**	Woe unto you, scribes and Pharisees, hypocrites! for ye make clean the outside of the cup and of the platter, but within they are full of extortion and excess.
Matt. 23:26	Thou blind Pharisee, cleanse first that which is within the cup and platter, that the outside of them may be clean also.
Matt. 23:27a **Matt. 23:27b**	Woe unto you, scribes and Pharisees, hypocrites! for ye are like unto whited sepulchres, which indeed appear beautiful outward, but are within full of dead men's bones, and of all uncleanness.
Matt. 23:28	Even so ye also outwardly appear righteous unto men, but within ye are full of hypocrisy and iniquity.
Matt. 23:29	Woe unto you, scribes and Pharisees, hypocrites! because ye build the tombs of the prophets, and garnish the sepulchres of the righteous,
Matt. 23:30	And say, If we had been in the days of our fathers, we would not have been partakers with them in the blood of the prophets.
Matt. 23:31	Wherefore ye be witnesses unto yourselves, that ye are the children of them which killed the prophets.

Matt. 23:32	Fill ye up then the measure of your fathers.
Matt. 23:33	Ye serpents, ye generation of vipers, how can ye escape the damnation of hell?
Matt. 23:34a Matt. 23:34b	¶ Wherefore, behold, I send unto you prophets, and wise men, and scribes: and some of them ye shall kill and crucify; and some of them shall ye scourge in your synagogues, and persecute them from city to city:
Matt. 23:35a Matt. 23:35b	That upon you may come all the righteous blood shed upon the earth, from the blood of righteous Abel unto the blood of Zechariah son of Barachias, whom ye slew between the temple and the altar.
Matt. 23:36	Verily I say unto you, All these things shall come upon this generation.
Matt. 23:37a Matt. 23:37b	O Jerusalem, Jerusalem, thou that killest the prophets, and stonest them which are sent unto thee, how often would I have gathered thy children together, even as a hen gathereth her chickens under her wings, and ye would not!
Matt. 23:38	Behold, your house is left unto you desolate.
Matt. 23:39	For I say unto you, Ye shall not see me henceforth, till ye shall say, Blessed is he that cometh in the name of the Lord.

18. A Certain Poor Widow
Mark 12:41–44; Luke 21:1–4

Mark 12:41a	¶ And Jesus sat over against the treasury, and beheld how the people cast money
Luke 21:1a	And he looked up, and saw the rich men casting their gifts
Mark 12:41b	into the treasury: and many that were rich cast in much.
Luke 21:1b	into the treasury.
Mark 12:42	And there came a certain poor widow, and she threw in two mites, which make a farthing.
Luke 21:2	And he saw also a certain poor widow casting in thither two mites.
Mark 12:43a	And he called unto him his disciples, and saith unto them, Verily I say unto you, That this poor widow hath cast more in,
Luke 21:3a	And he said, Of a truth I say unto you, that this poor widow hath cast in more
Mark 12:43b	than all they which have cast into the treasury:
Luke 21:3b	than they all
Mark 12:44a	For all they did cast in of their abundance; but she of her want did cast in all that she had,
Luke 21:4a	For all these have [cast in] of their abundance † unto the offerings of God: but she of her penury hath cast in all ‡ that she had
Mark 12:44b	even all her living.
Luke 21:4a	[the living].

19. Except a Corn of Wheat Fall
John 12:20–36a

John 12:20	¶ And there were certain Greeks among them that came up to worship at the feast:
John 12:21	The same came therefore to Philip, which was of Bethsaida of Galilee, and desired him, saying, Sir, we would see Jesus.
John 12:22	Philip cometh and telleth Andrew: and again Andrew and Philip tell Jesus.
John 12:23	¶ And Jesus answered them, saying, The hour is come, that the Son of man should be glorified.

John 12:24	Verily, verily, I say unto you, Except a corn of wheat fall into the ground and die, it abideth alone: but if it die, it bringeth forth much fruit.
John 12:25	He that loveth his life shall lose it; and he that hateth his life in this world shall keep it unto life eternal.
John 12:26	If any man serve me, let him follow me; and where I am, there shall also my servant be: if any man serve me, him will my Father honour.
John 12:27	Now is my soul troubled; and what shall I say? Father, save me from this hour: but for this cause came I unto this hour.
John 12:28	Father, glorify thy name. Then came there a voice from heaven, saying, I have both glorified it, and will glorify it again.
John 12:29	The people therefore, that stood by, and heard it, said that it thundered: others said, An angel spake to him.
John 12:30	Jesus answered and said, This voice came not because of me, but for your sakes.
John 12:31	Now is the judgment of this world: now shall the prince of this world be cast out.
John 12:32	And I, if I be lifted up from the earth, will draw all men unto me.
John 12:33	This he said, signifying what death he should die.
John 12:34a John 12:34b	The people answered him, We have heard out of the law that Christ abideth for ever: and how sayest thou, The Son of man must be lifted up? who is this Son of man?
John 12:35a John 12:35b	Then Jesus said unto them, Yet a little while is the light with you. Walk while ye have the light, lest darkness come upon you: for he that walketh in darkness knoweth not whither he goeth.
John 12:36a	While ye have light, believe in the light, that ye may be the children of light.

20. Yet They Believed Not on Him
John 12:36b–43

John 12:36b	These things spake Jesus, and departed, and did hide himself from them.
John 12:37	¶ But though he had done so many miracles before them, yet they believed not on him:
John 12:38a Isaiah 53:1a	That the saying of Esaias the prophet might be fulfilled, which he spake, Lord, who hath believed our report? Who hath believed our report?

John 12:38b	and to whom	hath	the arm of the Lord been		revealed?
Isaiah 53:1b	and to whom	is	the arm of the Lord		revealed?
John 12:39	Therefore they could not believe, because that Esaias said again,				
John 12:40a	He hath	blinded their eyes, and hardened their heart;		that they should not	see with their eyes,
Isaiah 6:10b		shut	their eyes;	lest they	see with their eyes,
John 12:40b	nor understand with their heart,	and be	converted,	and	I should	heal	them.
Isaiah 6:10c	and understand with their heart,	and	convert,	and		be	healed.
John 12:41	These things said Esaias, when he saw his glory, and spake of him.				
John 12:42a	¶ Nevertheless among the chief rulers also many believed on him; but because of the Pharisees they did not confess him,				
John 12:42b	lest they should be put out of the synagogue:				
John 12:43	For they loved the praise of men more than the praise of God.				

21. I Am Come a Light into the World

John 12:44–50

John 12:44	¶ Jesus cried and said, He that believeth on me, believeth not on me, but on him that sent me.
John 12:45	And he that seeth me seeth him that sent me.
John 12:46	I am come a light into the world, that whosoever believeth on me should not abide in darkness.
John 12:47	And if any man hear my words, and believe not, I judge him not: for I came not to judge the world, but to save the world.
John 12:48	He that rejecteth me, and receiveth not my words, hath one that judgeth him: the word that I have spoken, the same shall judge him in the last day.
John 12:49	For I have not spoken of myself; but the Father which sent me, he gave me a commandment, what I should say, and what I should speak.
John 12:50	And I know that his commandment is life everlasting: whatsoever I speak therefore, even as the Father said unto me, so I speak.

22. There Shall Not Be Left One Stone upon Another

Matt. 24:1–2; Mark 13:1–2; Luke 21:5–6

Matt. 24:1	And Jesus went out, and departed from the temple: and his disciples came to him for to shew him the buildings of the temple.
Mark 13:1a	And as he went out of the temple,
Mark 13:1b	one of his disciples saith unto him, Master, see what manner of stones and what buildings are here!
Luke 21:5a	¶ And as some spake of the temple, how it was adorned with goodly stones and gifts,
Matt. 24:2a	And Jesus said unto them,
Mark 13:2a	And Jesus answering said unto him,
Luke 21:5b	he said
Matt. 24:2b	See ye not all these things?
Mark 13:2b	Seest thou these great buildings?
Luke 21:6a	As for † which ye behold, [these things]
Matt. 24:2c	verily I say unto you, There shall not be left here one stone upon another, that shall not be thrown down.
Mark 13:2c	there shall not be left one stone upon another, that shall not be thrown down.
Luke 21:6b	the days will come, in the which there shall not be left one stone upon another, that shall not be thrown down.

23. What Shall Be the Sign of Thy Coming?

Matt. 24:3–8; Mark 13:3–8; Luke 21:7–19

Matt. 24:3a	¶ And as he sat upon the mount of Olives, the disciples came unto him privately,
Mark 13:3	And as he sat upon the mount of Olives over against the temple, Peter and James and John and Andrew asked him privately,
Luke 21:7a	And they asked him,
Matt. 24:3b	saying, Tell us, when shall these things be? and what shall be the sign of thy coming,
Mark 13:4a	Tell us, when shall these things be? and what shall be the sign
Luke 21:7b	saying, Master, but when shall these things be? and what sign will there be
Matt. 24:3c	and of the end of the world?
Mark 13:4b	when all these things shall be fulfilled?
Luke 21:7c	when these things shall come to pass?

Matt. 24:4	And Jesus answered and said unto them, Take heed that no man deceive you.
Mark 13:5	And Jesus answering them began to say, Take heed lest any man deceive you:
Luke 21:8a	And he said, Take heed that ye be not deceived:
Matt. 24:5	For many shall come in my name, saying, I am Christ; and shall deceive many.
Mark 13:6	For many shall come in my name, saying, I am Christ; and shall deceive many.
Luke 21:8b	for many shall come in my name, saying, I am Christ; and the time draweth near: go ye not therefore after them.
Matt. 24:6a	And ye shall hear of wars and rumours of wars: see that ye be not troubled:
Mark 13:7a	And when ye shall hear of wars and rumours of wars, be ye not troubled:
Luke 21:9a	But when ye shall hear of wars and commotions, be not terrified:
Matt. 24:6b	for all these things must come to pass, but the end is not yet.
Mark 13:7b	for such things must needs be; but the end shall not be yet.
Luke 21:9b	for these things must first come to pass; but the end is not by and by.
Matt. 24:7a	For nation shall rise against nation, and kingdom against kingdom:
Mark 13:8a	For nation shall rise against nation, and kingdom against kingdom:
Luke 21:10	Then said he unto them, Nation shall rise against nation, and kingdom against kingdom:
Matt. 24:7b	and there shall be [earthquakes,] ‡ [in divers places.] [famines,] and pestilences,
Mark 13:8b	and there shall be earthquakes in divers places, and there shall be famines and † * troubles:
Luke 21:11a	And shall be great earthquakes † in divers places, and famines, and pestilences;
Matt. 24:8	All these are the beginning of sorrows.
Mark 13:8c	these are the beginnings of sorrows.
Luke 21:11b	and fearful sights and great signs shall there be from heaven.

24. The Gospel Must First Be Published
Matt. 24:9–13; Mark 13:9–13; Luke 21:12–19

Matt. 24:9a	Then shall they deliver you up to be afflicted,
Mark 13:9a	¶ But take heed to yourselves: for they shall deliver you up to councils;
Luke 21:12a	But before all these, they shall lay their hands on you,
Matt. 24:9b	and shall kill you:
Mark 13:9b	and in the synagogues ye shall be beaten:

Luke 21:12b — and persecute you, delivering you up to the synagogues, and into prisons,

Matt. 24:9c — and ye shall be hated of all nations for my name's sake.

Mark 13:9c — and ye shall be brought before rulers and kings for my sake,

Luke 21:12c — being brought before kings and rulers for my name's sake.

Mark 13:13a — And ye shall be hated of all men for my name's sake:

Luke 21:17 — And ye shall be hated of all men for my name's sake.

Mark 13:9d — for a testimony against them.

Luke 21:13 — And it shall turn to you for a testimony.

Mark 13:10 — And the gospel must first be published among all nations.

Mark 13:11a — But when they shall lead you, and deliver you up, take no thought beforehand what ye shall speak,

Luke 21:14a — Settle it therefore in your hearts, not to meditate before what ye shall answer:

Mark 13:11b — neither do ye premeditate: but whatsoever shall be given you in that hour, that speak ye: for it is not ye that speak, but the Holy Ghost.

Luke 21:15 — For I will give you a mouth and wisdom, which all your adversaries shall not be able to gainsay nor resist.

Matt. 24:10a — And then shall many be offended, and shall betray one another,

Mark 13:12a — Now the brother shall betray the brother to death,

Luke 21:16a — And ye shall be betrayed both by parents, and brethren,

Matt. 24:10b — and shall hate one another.

Mark 13:12b — and the father the son; and children shall rise up against their parents,

Luke 21:16b — and kinsfolks, and friends;

Mark 13:12c — and shall cause them to be put to death.

Luke 21:16c — and some of you shall they cause to be put to death.

Matt. 24:11 — And many false prophets shall rise, and shall deceive many.

Matt. 24:12 — And because iniquity shall abound, the love of many shall wax cold.

Luke 21:18 — But there shall not an hair of your head perish.

Matt. 24:13 — But he that shall endure unto the end, the same shall be saved.

Mark 13:13b   but he that shall endure unto the end, the same shall be saved.

Luke 21:19   In your patience possess ye your souls.

25. The Abomination of Desolation
Matt. 24:15–21; Mark 13:14–19; Luke 21:20–24

Matt. 24:15a   When ye therefore shall see   the abomination of desolation,
Mark 13:14a   ¶ But when ye shall see   the abomination of desolation,
Luke 21:20   And when ye shall see Jerusalem compassed with armies, then know that the desolation thereof is nigh.

Matt. 24:15b   spoken of by Daniel the prophet, stand in the holy place,   (whoso readeth, let him understand:)
Mark 13:14b   spoken of by Daniel the prophet, standing   where it ought not,   [that readeth] let him † understand,)

Matt. 24:16   Then let them which be in Judaea flee into the mountains:
Mark 13:14b   then let them that be in Judaea flee to the mountains:
Luke 21:21a   Then let them which are in Judaea flee to the mountains;

Matt. 24:17   Let him which is on the housetop not come down   to take any thing out of his house:
Mark 13:15   And let him that is on the housetop not go down into the house, neither enter therein, to take any thing out of his house:

Luke 21:21b   and let them which are in the midst of it depart out; and let not them that are in the countries enter thereinto.

Matt. 24:18   Neither let him which is in the field return back to take his clothes.
Mark 13:16   And let him that is in the field not turn back again for to take up his garment.

Luke 21:22   For these be the days of vengeance, that all things which are written may be fulfilled.

Matt. 24:19   And woe unto them that are with child, and to them that give suck in those days!
Mark 13:17   But woe to them that are with child, and to them that give suck in those days!
Luke 21:23a   But woe unto them that are with child, and to them that give suck, in those days!

Matt. 24:20   But pray ye that your flight be not in the winter, neither on the sabbath day:
Mark 13:18   And pray ye that your flight be not in the winter.

Matt. 24:21a   For then shall be great tribulation,
Mark 13:19a   For in those days shall be affliction,

Luke 21:23b for   there shall be great distress   in the land, and wrath upon this people.

Matt. 24:21b such as was not since the beginning of the world   to   this time, no, nor ever shall be.

Mark 13:19b such as was not from the beginning of the creation which God created unto this time, neither   shall be.

Luke 21:24a And they shall fall by the edge of the sword, and shall be led away captive into all nations: and Jerusalem shall be trodden down of the Gentiles,

Luke 21:24b until the times of the Gentiles be fulfilled.

26. Except Those Days Be Shortened

Matt. 24:22–28; Mark 13:20–23

Matt. 24:22a And except † should be shortened [those days], there should no flesh be saved:
Mark 13:20a And except that the Lord had shortened those days, [should] no flesh † be saved:

Matt. 24:22b but for the elect's sake those days shall be shortened.
Mark 13:20b but for the elect's sake, whom he hath chosen, he hath [the days] shortened†.

Matt. 24:23 Then if any man shall say unto you, Lo, here is Christ, or there; believe it not.
Mark 13:21 And then if any man shall say to you, Lo, here is Christ; or, lo, he is there; believe him not:

Matt. 24:24a For there shall arise false Christs, and false prophets, and shall shew great signs and wonders;
Mark 13:22a For [shall arise] false Christs and false prophets†, and shall shew signs and wonders,

Matt. 24:24b insomuch that, if it were possible, they shall deceive the very elect.
Mark 13:22b † if it were possible, [to seduce,] even the elect.

Matt. 24:25 Behold, I have told you before.
Mark 13:23 But take ye heed: behold, I have foretold you all things.

Matt. 24:26 Wherefore if they shall say unto you, Behold, he is in the desert; go not forth: behold, he is in the secret chambers; believe it not.

Matt. 24:27 For as the lightning cometh out of the east, and shineth even unto the west; so shall also the coming of the Son of man be.

Matt. 24:28 For wheresoever the carcase is, there will the eagles be gathered together.

27. After the Tribulation of Those Days

Matt. 24:29–31; Mark 13:24–27; Luke 21:25–28

Matt. 24:29a Immediately after the tribulation of those days † the sun [shall] be darkened,
Mark 13:24a ¶ But † after that tribulation [in those days,], the sun shall be darkened,
Luke 21:25a ¶ And there shall be signs in the sun,

Matt. 24:29b and the moon shall not give her light,

Mark 13:24b	and	the moon shall not give her light,
Luke 21:25b	and in	the moon,

Matt. 24:29c	and	the stars shall fall from heaven, and the powers of the	heavens	shall be shaken:
Mark 13:25	And	the stars [shall fall] of heaven †, and the powers that are in heaven		shall be shaken.
Luke 21:25c	and in	the stars; and upon the earth distress of nations,		

Luke 21:25d — with perplexity; the sea and the waves roaring;

Matt. 24:30a — And then shall appear the sign of the Son of man in heaven: and then shall all the tribes of the earth mourn,

Matt. 24:30b	and	they shall see the Son of man coming in the	clouds of heaven	with power and great glory.
Mark 13:26	And then	shall they see the Son of man coming in the	clouds	with †power and [great] glory.
Luke 21:27	And then	shall they see the Son of man coming in a	cloud	with power and great glory.

Matt. 24:31a	And	he shall send his angels with a great sound of a trumpet, and they	shall gather together his elect from the four winds,
Mark 13:27a	And then	shall he send his angels, and	shall gather together his elect from the four winds,

Matt. 24:31b	from		one end	of heaven to the other.
Mark 13:27b	from the uttermost part of the earth	to the uttermost	part	of heaven.

Luke 21:28 — And when these things begin to come to pass, then look up, and lift up your heads; for your redemption draweth nigh.

28. This Generation Shall Not Pass

Matt. 24:34–35; Mark 13:30–31; Luke 21:32–33

Matt. 24:34	Verily I say unto you,	This generation	shall not pass,	till all these things be fulfilled.
Mark 13:30	Verily I say unto you, that	this generation	shall not pass,	till all these things be done.
Luke 21:32	Verily I say unto you,	This generation	shall not pass away,	till all be fulfilled.

Matt. 24:35	Heaven and earth shall pass away, but my words shall not pass away.
Mark 13:31	Heaven and earth shall pass away: but my words shall not pass away.
Luke 21:33	Heaven and earth shall pass away: but my words shall not pass away.

29. Parable of the Fig Tree
Matt. 24:32–33; Mark 13:28–29; Luke 21:29–31

Matt. 24:32a	Now learn a parable of the fig tree;
Mark 13:28a	Now learn a parable of the fig tree;
Luke 21:29a	And he spake to them a parable; Behold the fig tree, and all the trees;

Matt. 24:32b	When his branch is yet tender, and putteth forth leaves, ye know that summer is nigh:
Mark 13:28b	When her branch is yet tender, and putteth forth leaves, ye know that summer is near:
Luke 21:30a	When they now shoot forth, ye see and know of your own selves that summer is now nigh at hand.

Matt. 24:33	So likewise ye, when ye shall see all these things, know that it is near,
Mark 13:11	So † in like manner [ye], when ye shall see these things come to pass, know that it is nigh,
Luke 21:11	So likewise ye, when ye see these things come to pass, know ye that the kingdom of God is nigh at hand.

Matt. 24:33b	even at the doors.
Mark 13:11b	even at the doors.

30. That Day and Hour Knoweth No Man
Matt. 24:36; Mark 13:32

Matt. 24:36	¶ But of that day and hour knoweth no man, no, not the angels of heaven, but my Father only.
Mark 13:32	¶ But of that day and that hour knoweth no man, no, not the angels which are in heaven, neither the Son, but the Father.

31. So Shall Also The Coming of the Son of Man Be
Matt. 24:37–42; Mark 13:13; Luke 21:34–36

Matt. 24:37	But as the days of Noe were, so shall also the coming of the Son of man be.
Matt. 24:38a	For as in the days that were before the flood they were eating and drinking, marrying and giving in marriage,
Matt. 24:38b	until the day that Noe entered into the ark,
Matt. 24:39	And knew not until the flood came, and took them all away; so shall also the coming of the Son of man be.

Matt. 24:40	Then shall two be in the field; the one shall be taken, and the other left.
Matt. 24:41	Two women shall be grinding at the mill; the one shall be taken, and the other left.
Luke 21:34a	And take heed to yourselves, lest at any time your hearts be overcharged with surfeiting, and drunkenness, and cares of this life,
Luke 21:34b	and so that day come upon you unawares.
Luke 21:35	For as a snare shall it come on all them that dwell on the face of the whole earth.
Matt. 24:42a	Watch therefore:
Mark 13:33a	Take ye heed, watch and pray:
Luke 21:36a	Watch ye therefore, and pray always,
Luke 21:36b	that ye may be accounted worthy to escape all these things that shall come to pass, and to stand before the Son of man.
Matt. 24:42b	for ye know not what hour your Lord doth come.
Mark 13:33b	for ye know not when the time is.

32. A Man Taking a Far Journey
Mark 13:34–37

Mark 13:34a	For the Son of man is as a man taking a far journey, who left his house, and gave authority to his servants, and to every man his work,
Mark 13:34b	and commanded the porter to watch.
Mark 13:35	Watch ye therefore: for ye know not when the master of the house cometh, at even, or at midnight, or at the cockcrowing, or in the morning:
Mark 13:36	Lest coming suddenly he find you sleeping.
Mark 13:37	And what I say unto you I say unto all, Watch.

33. Who Then Is a Faithful and a Wise Servant?
Matthew 24:43–51

| Matt. 24:43a | But know this, that if the goodman of the house had known in what watch the thief would come, he would have watched, and |
| Matt. 24:43b | would not have suffered his house to be broken up. |

Matt. 24:44   Therefore be ye also ready: for in such an hour as ye think not the Son of man cometh.

Matt. 24:45   Who then is a faithful and wise servant, whom his lord hath made ruler over his household, to give them meat in due season?

Matt. 24:46   Blessed is that servant, whom his lord when he cometh shall find so doing.

Matt. 24:47   Verily I say unto you, That he shall make him ruler over all his goods.

Matt. 24:48   But and if that evil servant shall say in his heart, My lord delayeth his coming;

Matt. 24:49   And shall begin to smite his fellowservants, and to eat and drink with the drunken;

Matt. 24:50   The lord of that servant shall come in a day when he looketh not for him, and in an hour that he is not aware of,

Matt. 24:51   And shall cut him asunder, and appoint him his portion with the hypocrites: there shall be weeping and gnashing of teeth.

34. Five of Them Were Wise, and Five Were Foolish
Matthew 25:1–13

Matt. 25:1   Then shall the kingdom of heaven be likened unto ten virgins, which took their lamps, and went forth to meet the bridegroom.

Matt. 25:2   And five of them were wise, and five were foolish.

Matt. 25:3   They that were foolish took their lamps, and took no oil with them:

Matt. 25:4   But the wise took oil in their vessels with their lamps.

Matt. 25:5   While the bridegroom tarried, they all slumbered and slept.

Matt. 25:6   And at midnight there was a cry made, Behold, the bridegroom cometh; go ye out to meet him.

Matt. 25:7   Then all those virgins arose, and trimmed their lamps.

Matt. 25:8   And the foolish said unto the wise, Give us of your oil; for our lamps are gone out.

Matt. 25:9   But the wise answered, saying, Not so; lest there be not enough for us and you: but go ye rather to them that sell, and buy for yourselves.

Matt. 25:10 And while they went to buy, the bridegroom came; and they that were ready went in with him to the marriage: and the door was shut.

Matt. 25:11 Afterward came also the other virgins, saying, Lord, Lord, open to us.

Matt. 25:12 But he answered and said, Verily I say unto you, I know you not.

Matt. 25:13 Watch therefore, for ye know neither the day nor the hour wherein the Son of man cometh.

35. Well Done, Thou Good and Faithful Servant
Matthew 25:14–30

Matt. 25:14 ¶ For the kingdom of heaven is as a man travelling into a far country, who called his own servants, and delivered unto them his goods.

Matt. 25:15a And unto one he gave five talents, to another two, and to another one; to every man according to his several ability; and straightway
Matt. 25:15b took his journey.

Matt. 25:16 Then he that had received the five talents went and traded with the same, and made them other five talents.

Matt. 25:17 And likewise he that had received two, he also gained other two.

Matt. 25:18 But he that had received one went and digged in the earth, and hid his lord's money.

Matt. 25:19 After a long time the lord of those servants cometh, and reckoneth with them.

Matt. 25:20a And so he that had received five talents came and brought other five talents, saying, Lord, thou deliveredst unto me five talents: behold,
Matt. 25:20b I have gained beside them five talents more.

Matt. 25:21a His lord said unto him, Well done, thou good and faithful servant: thou hast been faithful over a few things, I will make thee ruler over many things:
Matt. 25:21b enter thou into the joy of thy lord.

Matt. 25:22a He also that had received two talents came and said, Lord, thou deliveredst unto me two talents: behold, I have gained two other talents
Matt. 25:22b beside them.

Matt. 25:23a His lord said unto him, Well done, good and faithful servant; thou hast been faithful over a few things, I will make thee ruler over many things:
Matt. 25:23b enter thou into the joy of thy lord.

Matt. 25:24a Then he which had received the one talent came and said, Lord, I knew thee that thou art an hard man, reaping where thou hast not sown,
Matt. 25:24b and gathering where thou hast not strawed:

Matt. 25:25 And I was afraid, and went and hid thy talent in the earth: lo, there thou hast that is thine.

Matt. 25:26a His lord answered and said unto him, Thou wicked and slothful servant, thou knewest that I reap where I sowed not, and gather where
Matt. 25:26b I have not strawed:

Matt. 25:27 Thou oughtest therefore to have put my money to the exchangers, and then at my coming I should have received mine own with usury.

Matt. 25:28 Take therefore the talent from him, and give it unto him which hath ten talents.

Matt. 25:29 For unto every one that hath shall be given, and he shall have abundance: but from him that hath not shall be taken away even that which he hath.

Matt. 25:30 And cast ye the unprofitable servant into outer darkness: there shall be weeping and gnashing of teeth.

36. Unto the Least of These My Brethren
Matthew 25:31–46

Matt. 25:31 ¶ When the Son of man shall come in his glory, and all the holy angels with him, then shall he sit upon the throne of his glory:

Matt. 25:32 And before him shall be gathered all nations: and he shall separate them one from another, as a shepherd divideth his sheep from the goats:

Matt. 25:33 And he shall set the sheep on his right hand, but the goats on the left.

Matt. 25:34a Then shall the King say unto them on his right hand, Come, ye blessed of my Father, inherit the kingdom prepared for you from the
Matt. 25:34b foundation of the world:

Matt. 25:35 For I was an hungred, and ye gave me meat: I was thirsty, and ye gave me drink: I was a stranger, and ye took me in:

Matt. 25:36 Naked, and ye clothed me: I was sick, and ye visited me: I was in prison, and ye came unto me.

Matt. 25:37 Then shall the righteous answer him, saying, Lord, when saw we thee an hungred, and fed thee? or thirsty, and gave thee drink?

Matt. 25:38 When saw we thee a stranger, and took thee in? or naked, and clothed thee?

Matt. 25:39 Or when saw we thee sick, or in prison, and came unto thee?

Matt. 25:40a
Matt. 25:40b And the King shall answer and say unto them, Verily I say unto you, Inasmuch as ye have done it unto one of the least of these my brethren, ye have done it unto me.

Matt. 25:41 Then shall he say also unto them on the left hand, Depart from me, ye cursed, into everlasting fire, prepared for the devil and his angels:

Matt. 25:42 For I was an hungred, and ye gave me no meat: I was thirsty, and ye gave me no drink:

Matt. 25:43 I was a stranger, and ye took me not in: naked, and ye clothed me not: sick, and in prison, and ye visited me not.

Matt. 25:44a
Matt. 25:44b Then shall they also answer him, saying, Lord, when saw we thee an hungred, or athirst, or a stranger, or naked, or sick, or in prison, and did not minister unto thee?

Matt. 25:45 Then shall he answer them, saying, Verily I say unto you, Inasmuch as ye did it not to one of the least of these, ye did it not to me.

Matt. 25:46 And these shall go away into everlasting punishment: but the righteous into life eternal.

37. Not on the Feast Day Lest There Be an Uproar among the People
Matt. 26:1–5; Mark 14:1–2; Luke 22:1–2

Matt. 26:1 And it came to pass, when Jesus had finished all these sayings, he said unto his disciples,

Matt. 26:2a Ye know that after two days is the passover,
Mark 14:1a After two days was the feast of the passover, and of unleavened bread:
Luke 22:1 Now the feast of [which is called the Passover.] unleavened bread drew nigh, †

Matt. 26:3a Then assembled together the chief priests, and the scribes, and the elders of the people,
Mark 14:1b and the chief priests and the scribes
Luke 22:2a And the chief priests and scribes

Matt. 26:3b unto the palace of the high priest, who was called Caiaphas,

Matt. 26:4 And consulted that they might take Jesus by subtilty, and kill him.
Mark 14:1b sought how they might take him by craft, and put him to death.
Luke 22:2b sought how they might kill him; for they feared the people.

Matt. 26:5 But they said, Not on the feast day, lest there be an uproar among the people.

Mark 14:2   But they said, Not on the feast day, lest there be an uproar of   the people.

38. What Will Ye Give Me and I Will Deliver Him unto You?

Matt. 26:14–16; Mark 14:10–11; Luke 22:3–6

Matt. 26:14a	¶ Then	one called	Judas	Iscariot,	[one of the twelve,]		
Mark 14:10a	¶ And		Judas	Iscariot,	one of the twelve,		
Luke 22:3	¶ Then entered Satan into		Judas surnamed	Iscariot, being	one of the twelve.		

Matt. 26:14b	went	unto	the chief priests	
Mark 14:10b	went	unto	the chief priests	to betray him unto them.
Luke 22:4	And he went his way, and communed with		the chief priests and captains, how he might	betray him unto them.

Matt. 26:15a   And said unto them, What will ye give me, and I will deliver him unto you?

Matt. 26:15b	And	they	covenanted	with him for	thirty pieces of silver.
Mark 14:11a	And when they heard it, they were glad, and	promised	to give	him	money.
Luke 22:5	And	they were glad, and	covenanted	to give	him	money.

Matt. 26:16	And from that time he	sought opportunity		to	betray him.
Mark 14:11b	And	he	sought		betray him.
Luke 22:6a	And	he promised,	and sought opportunity	how he might conveniently	to	betray him unto them

Luke 22:6b   in the absence of the multitude.

PART 5

The Fifth Day of the Week

Thursday

39. Go and Prepare Us the Passover

Matt. 26:17–20; Mark 14:12–16; Luke 22:7–13

Matt. 26:17a ¶Now the first day of the feast of unleavened bread
Mark 14:12a ¶And the first day of unleavened bread, when † the passover, [they killed]
Luke 22:7 ¶Then came the day of unleavened bread, when the passover must be killed.

Luke 22:8 And he sent Peter and John, saying, Go and prepare us the passover, that we may eat.

Matt. 26:17b the disciples came to Jesus, saying unto him,
Mark 14:12b his disciples said unto him,
Luke 22:9a And they said unto him,

Matt. 26:17c Where wilt thou that we prepare for thee to eat the passover?
Mark 14:12c Where wilt thou that we go and prepare that thou mayest eat the passover?
Luke 22:9b Where wilt thou that we prepare?

Matt. 26:18a And he said, Go into the city
Mark 14:13a And he sendeth forth two of his disciples, and saith unto them, Go ye into the city,
Luke 22:10a And he said unto them, Behold, when ye are entered into the city,

Matt. 26:18b to such a man, and
Mark 14:13b there shall meet you a man bearing a pitcher of water: follow him.
Luke 22:10b here shall † meet you, [a man] bearing a pitcher of water; follow him into the house where he entereth in.

Matt. 26:18c and say unto him, The Master saith,
Mark 14:14a And wheresoever he shall go in, say ye to the goodman of the house, The Master saith,
Luke 22:11a And ye shall say unto the goodman of the house, The Master saith unto thee,

Matt. 26:18d My time is at hand; I will keep the passover at thy house with my disciples.
Mark 14:14b Where is the guestchamber, where I shall eat the passover with my disciples?
Luke 22:11b Where is the guestchamber, where I shall eat the passover with my disciples?

Mark 14:15 And he will shew you a large upper room furnished and prepared: there make ready for us.
Luke 22:12 And he shall shew you a large upper room furnished: there make ready.

Matt. 19:20a	And the disciples did as Jesus had appointed them;						
Mark 14:16a	And his disciples	went forth, and came into the city,	and found as he had said unto them:				
Luke 22:13a	And they	went,	and found as he had said unto them:				

Matt. 19:20b	and they made ready the passover.
Mark 14:16b	and they made ready the passover.
Luke 22:13b	and they made ready the passover.

40. With Desire I Have Desired to Eat This Passover with You

Matt. 26:20; Mark 14:17; Luke 22:14–18

Matt. 26:20	Now when	[was come]	the even[,	he	sat down	with	the twelve.
Mark 14:17	And		in	the evening	he cometh	with	the twelve.
Luke 22:14	And when the hour was come,			he	sat down, and		the twelve apostles with him.

Luke 22:15	And he said unto them, With desire I have desired to eat this passover with you before I suffer:
Luke 22:16	For I say unto you, I will not any more eat thereof, until it be fulfilled in the kingdom of God.
Luke 22:17	And he took the cup, and gave thanks, and said, Take this, and divide it among yourselves:
Luke 22:18	For I say unto you, I will not drink of the fruit of the vine, until the kingdom of God shall come.

41. There Was Also a Strife among Them

Luke 22:24–30

Luke 22:24	¶ And there was also a strife among them, which of them should be accounted the greatest.
Luke 22:25	And he said unto them, The kings of the Gentiles exercise lordship over them; and they that exercise authority upon them are called benefactors.
Luke 22:26	But ye shall not be so: but he that is greatest among you, let him be as the younger; and he that is chief, as he that doth serve.
Luke 22:27	For whether is greater, he that sitteth at meat, or he that serveth? is not he that sitteth at meat? but I am among you as he that serveth.
Luke 22:28	Ye are they which have continued with me in my temptations.

Luke 22:29   And I appoint unto you a kingdom, as my Father hath appointed unto me;

Luke 22:30   That ye may eat and drink at my table in my kingdom, and sit on thrones judging the twelve tribes of Israel.

42. For I Have Given You an Example
John 13:1–20; Psalms 41:9

John 13:1a   Now before the feast of the passover, when Jesus knew that his hour was come that he should depart out of this world unto the Father,
John 13:1b   having loved his own which were in the world, he loved them unto the end.

John 13:2   And supper being ended, the devil having now put into the heart of Judas Iscariot, Simon's son, to betray him;

John 13:3   Jesus knowing that the Father had given all things into his hands, and that he was come from God, and went to God;

John 13:4   He riseth from supper, and laid aside his garments; and took a towel, and girded himself.

John 13:5   After that he poureth water into a bason, and began to wash the disciples' feet, and to wipe them with the towel wherewith he was girded.

John 13:6   Then cometh he to Simon Peter: and Peter saith unto him, Lord, dost thou wash my feet?

John 13:7   Jesus answered and said unto him, What I do thou knowest not now; but thou shalt know hereafter.

John 13:8   Peter saith unto him, Thou shalt never wash my feet. Jesus answered him, If I wash thee not, thou hast no part with me.

John 13:9   Simon Peter saith unto him, Lord, not my feet only, but also my hands and my head.

John 13:10   Jesus saith to him, He that is washed needeth not save to wash his feet, but is clean every whit: and ye are clean, but not all.

John 13:11   For he knew who should betray him; therefore said he, Ye are not all clean.

John 13:12   So after he had washed their feet, and had taken his garments, and was set down again, he said unto them, Know ye what I have done to you?

John 13:13   Ye call me Master and Lord: and ye say well; for so I am.

John 13:14   If I then, your Lord and Master, have washed your feet; ye also ought to wash one another's feet.

John 13:15   For I have given you an example, that ye should do as I have done to you.

John 13:16	Verily, verily, I say unto you, The servant is not greater than his lord; neither he that is sent greater than he that sent him.
John 13:17	If ye know these things, happy are ye if ye do them.
John 13:18a	¶ I speak not of you all: I know whom I have chosen: but that the scripture may be fulfilled,
John 13:18b	He that eateth bread with me hath lifted up his heel against me.
Psalms 41:9	Yea, mine own familiar friend, in whom I trusted, which did eat of my bread, hath lifted up his heel against me.
John 13:19	Now I tell you before it come, that, when it is come to pass, ye may believe that I am he.
John 13:20	Verily, verily, I say unto you, He that receiveth whomsoever I send receiveth me; and he that receiveth me receiveth him that sent me.

43. One of You Shall Betray Me

Matt. 26:21–25; Mark 14:18–21; Luke 22:21–23; John 13:21–22

Matt. 26:21a	And as they did eat, he said,
Mark 14:18a	And as they sat and did eat, Jesus said,
John 13:21a	When Jesus had thus said, he was troubled in spirit, and testified, and said,
Matt. 26:21b	Verily I say unto you, that one of you shall betray me.
Mark 14:18b	Verily I say unto you, One of you which eateth with me shall betray me.
Luke 22:21a	¶ But, behold,
John 13:21b	Verily, verily, I say unto you, that one of you shall betray me.
Luke 22:21b	the hand of him that betrayeth me is with me on the table.
John 13:22	Then the disciples looked one on another, doubting of whom he spake.
Luke 22:23	And they began to enquire among themselves, which of them it was that should do this thing.
Matt. 26:22	And they were exceeding sorrowful, and began every one of them to say unto him, Lord, is it I?
Mark 14:19	And they began to be sorrowful, and [one by one] to say unto him], Is it I? and another said, Is it I?
Matt. 26:23	And he answered and said, He that dippeth his hand with me in the dish, the same shall betray me.
Mark 14:20	And he answered and said unto them, It is one of the twelve, that dippeth with me in the dish.

Matt. 26:24a	The Son of man	goeth as it is written	of him: but woe unto	that man by whom the Son of man	is betrayed!
Mark 14:21a	The Son of man indeed	goeth, as it is written	of him: but woe to	that man by whom the Son of man	is betrayed!
Luke 22:22	And truly the Son of man	goeth, as it was determined:	but woe unto	that man by whom he	is betrayed!

Matt. 26:24b	it had been good	for that man if he had not	been born.
Mark 14:21b	good were it	for that man if he had never	been born.

Matt. 26:25   Then Judas, which betrayed him, answered and said, Master, is it I? He said unto him, Thou hast said.

44. That Thou Doest, Do Quickly
John 13:23–30

John 13:23   Now there was leaning on Jesus' bosom one of his disciples, whom Jesus loved.

John 13:24   Simon Peter therefore beckoned to him, that he should ask who it should be of whom he spake.

John 13:25   He then lying on Jesus' breast saith unto him, Lord, who is it?

John 13:26a
John 13:26b   Jesus answered, He it is, to whom I shall give a sop, when I have dipped it. And when he had dipped the sop, he gave it to Judas Iscariot, the son of Simon.

John 13:27   And after the sop Satan entered into him. Then said Jesus unto him, That thou doest, do quickly.

John 13:28   Now no man at the table knew for what intent he spake this unto him.

John 13:29a
John 13:29b   For some of them thought, because Judas had the bag, that Jesus had said unto him, Buy those things that we have need of against the feast; or, that he should give something to the poor.

John 13:30   He then having received the sop went immediately out: and it was night.

45. Love One Another
John 13:31–35

John 13:31   ¶ Therefore, when he was gone out, Jesus said, Now is the Son of man glorified, and God is glorified in him.

John 13:32 — If God be glorified in him, God shall also glorify him in himself, and shall straightway glorify him.

John 13:33 — Little children, yet a little while I am with you. Ye shall seek me: and as I said unto the Jews, Whither I go, ye cannot come; so now I say to you.

John 13:34 — A new commandment I give unto you, That ye love one another; as I have loved you, that ye also love one another.

John 13:35 — By this shall all men know that ye are my disciples, if ye have love one to another.

46. Jesus Took Bread and Blessed It

Matt. 26:26–29; Mark 14:22–25; Luke 22:19–20

Matt. 26:26a	¶ And as they were eating, Jesus took bread, and blessed it, and brake it, and gave it to the disciples,
Mark 14:22a	¶ And as they did eat, Jesus took bread, and blessed, and brake it, and gave to them,
Luke 22:19a	¶ And he took bread, and gave thanks, and brake it, and gave unto them,
Matt. 26:26b	and said, Take, eat; this is my body.
Mark 14:22b	and said, Take, eat: this is my body.
Luke 22:19b	saying, This is my body which is given for you: this do in remembrance of me.
Matt. 26:27	And he took the cup, and gave thanks, and gave it to them, saying, Drink ye all of it;
Mark 14:23a	And he took the cup, and when he had given thanks, he gave it to them:
Luke 22:20a	Likewise also the cup after supper, saying
Mark 14:23b	and they all drank of it.
Matt. 26:28	For this is my blood of the new testament, which is shed for many for the remission of sins.
Mark 14:24	This is my blood of the new testament, which is shed for many.
Luke 22:20b	This cup is [in my blood] the new testament †, which is shed for you.
Matt. 26:29a	But I say unto you, I will not drink henceforth of this fruit of the vine,
Mark 26:25a	Verily I say unto you, I will [no more] drink † of the fruit of the vine,
Matt. 26:29b	until that day when I drink it new with you in my Father's kingdom.
Mark 14:25b	until that day that I drink it new in the kingdom of God.

47. Before the Cock Crow Twice

Matt. 26:31–35; Mark 14:27–31; Luke 22:31–38; John 13:36–38

Matt. 26:31a	Then saith Jesus unto them, All ye shall be offended because of me this night: for it is written,
Mark 14:27a	And Jesus saith unto them, All ye shall be offended because of me this night: for it is written,
Matt. 26:31b	I will smite the shepherd, and the sheep of the flock shall be scattered abroad.
Mark 14:27b	I will smite the shepherd, and the sheep shall be scattered.
Matt. 26:32	But after I am risen again, I will go before you into Galilee.
Mark 14:28	But after that I am risen, I will go before you into Galilee.
Matt. 26:33	Peter answered and said unto him, Though all men shall be offended because of thee, yet will I never be offended.
Mark 14:29	But Peter said unto him, Although all shall be offended, yet will not I.
Luke 22:31	¶ And the Lord said, Simon, Simon, behold, Satan hath desired to have you, that he may sift you as wheat:
Luke 22:32	But I have prayed for thee, that thy faith fail not: and when thou art converted, strengthen thy brethren.
John 13:36a	¶ Simon Peter said unto him, Lord, whither goest thou? Jesus answered him, Whither I go, thou canst not follow me now;
John 13:36b	but thou shalt follow me afterwards.
Luke 22:33	And he said unto him, Lord, I am ready to go with thee, both into prison, and to death.
John 13:37a	Peter said unto him, Lord, why cannot I follow thee now?
John 13:37b	I will lay down my life for thy sake.
Matt. 26:34a	Jesus said unto him, Verily I say unto thee, That this night,
Mark 14:30a	And Jesus saith unto him, Verily I say unto thee, That this day, even in this night,
Luke 22:34a	And he said, I tell thee, Peter,
John 13:38a	Jesus answered him, Wilt thou lay down thy life for my sake.
Matt. 26:34b	before the cock crow, thou shalt deny me thrice.
Mark 14:30b	before the cock crow twice, thou shalt deny me thrice.
Luke 22:34b	[before that] the cock shall not crow this day, † that thou shalt [deny] thrice † that thou knowest me.
John 13:38	Verily, verily, I say unto thee, The cock shall not crow, till thou hast denied me thrice.
Matt. 26:35a	Peter said unto him, Though I should die with thee, yet will I not deny thee.

Mark 14:31a	But he spake the more vehemently, If I should die with thee, I will not deny thee in any wise.
Matt. 26:35b	Likewise also said all the disciples.
Mark 14:31b	Likewise also said they all.
Luke 22:35	And he said unto them, When I sent you without purse, and scrip, and shoes, lacked ye any thing? And they said, Nothing.
Luke 22:36a	Then said he unto them, But now, he that hath a purse, let him take it, and likewise his scrip: and he that hath no sword,
Luke 22:36b	let him sell his garment, and buy one.
Luke 22:37a Isa. 53:12b	For I say unto you, that this that is written must yet be accomplished in me, And he was reckoned among the transgressors: and he was numbered with the transgressors;
Luke 22:37b	for the things concerning me have an end.
Luke 22:38	And they said, Lord, behold, here are two swords. And he said unto them, It is enough.

48. I Am the Way, the Truth, and the Life
John 14:1–31a

John 14:1	Let not your heart be troubled: ye believe in God, believe also in me.
John 14:2	In my Father's house are many mansions: if it were not so, I would have told you. I go to prepare a place for you.
John 14:3	And if I go and prepare a place for you, I will come again, and receive you unto myself; that where I am, there ye may be also.
John 14:4	And whither I go ye know, and the way ye know.
John 14:5	Thomas saith unto him, Lord, we know not whither thou goest; and how can we know the way?
John 14:6	Jesus saith unto him, I am the way, the truth, and the life: no man cometh unto the Father, but by me.
John 14:7	If ye had known me, ye should have known my Father also: and from henceforth ye know him, and have seen him.
John 14:8	Philip saith unto him, Lord, shew us the Father, and it sufficeth us.
John 14:9a	Jesus saith unto him, Have I been so long time with you, and yet hast thou not known me, Philip? he that hath seen me hath seen the

John 14:9b	Father; and how sayest thou then, Shew us the Father?
John 14:10a **John 14:10b**	Believest thou not that I am in the Father, and the Father in me? the words that I speak unto you I speak not of myself: but the Father that dwelleth in me, he doeth the works.
John 14:11	Believe me that I am in the Father, and the Father in me: or else believe me for the very works' sake.
John 14:12a **John 14:12b**	Verily, verily, I say unto you, He that believeth on me, the works that I do shall he do also; and greater works than these shall he do; because I go unto my Father.
John 14:13	And whatsoever ye shall ask in my name, that will I do, that the Father may be glorified in the Son.
John 14:14	If ye shall ask any thing in my name, I will do it.
John 14:15	¶ If ye love me, keep my commandments.
John 14:16	And I will pray the Father, and he shall give you another Comforter, that he may abide with you for ever;
John 14:17a **John 14:17b**	Even the Spirit of truth; whom the world cannot receive, because it seeth him not, neither knoweth him: but ye know him; for he dwelleth with you, and shall be in you.
John 14:18	I will not leave you comfortless: I will come to you.
John 14:19	Yet a little while, and the world seeth me no more; but ye see me: because I live, ye shall live also.
John 14:20	At that day ye shall know that I am in my Father, and ye in me, and I in you.
John 14:21a **John 14:21b**	He that hath my commandments, and keepeth them, he it is that loveth me: and he that loveth me shall be loved of my Father, and I will love him, and will manifest myself to him.
John 14:22	Judas saith unto him, not Iscariot, Lord, how is it that thou wilt manifest thyself unto us, and not unto the world?
John 14:23a **John 14:23b**	Jesus answered and said unto him, If a man love me, he will keep my words: and my Father will love him, and we will come unto him, and make our abode with him.
John 14:24	He that loveth me not keepeth not my sayings: and the word which ye hear is not mine, but the Father's which sent me.
John 14:25	These things have I spoken unto you, being yet present with you.

John 14:26a But the Comforter, which is the Holy Ghost, whom the Father will send in my name, he shall teach you all things, and bring all things
John 14:26b to your remembrance, whatsoever I have said unto you.

John 14:27 Peace I leave with you, my peace I give unto you: not as the world giveth, give I unto you. Let not your heart be troubled, neither let it be afraid.

John 14:28a Ye have heard how I said unto you, I go away, and come again unto you. If ye loved me, ye would rejoice, because I said, I go unto the Father:
John 14:28b for my Father is greater than I.

John 14:29 And now I have told you before it come to pass, that, when it is come to pass, ye might believe.

John 14:30 Hereafter I will not talk much with you: for the prince of this world cometh, and hath nothing in me.

John 14:31a But that the world may know that I love the Father; and as the Father gave me commandment, even so I do.

49. Arise, Let Us Go Hence

Matthew 26:30, Mark 14:26, Luke 22:39, John 14:31b

John 14:31a Arise, let us go hence.

Matt. 26:30a	And when they had sung an hymn,	they	went	out
Mark 14:26a	And when they had sung an hymn,	they	went	out
Luke 22:39a	And	he	[went,] ‡ and [came out,] †	as he was wont,

Matt. 26:30b	into	the mount of Olives.	
Mark 14:26b	into	the mount of Olives.	
Luke 22:39b	to	the mount of Olives;	and his disciples also followed him.

50. I Am the True Vine

John 15:1–27; Psalms 69:4

John 15:1 I am the true vine, and my Father is the husbandman.

John 15:2 Every branch in me that beareth not fruit he taketh away: and every branch that beareth fruit, he purgeth it, that it may bring forth more fruit.

John 15:3 Now ye are clean through the word which I have spoken unto you.

John 15:4	Abide in me, and I in you. As the branch cannot bear fruit of itself, except it abide in the vine; no more can ye, except ye abide in me.
John 15:5	I am the vine, ye are the branches: He that abideth in me, and I in him, the same bringeth forth much fruit: for without me ye can do nothing.
John 15:6	If a man abide not in me, he is cast forth as a branch, and is withered; and men gather them, and cast them into the fire, and they are burned.
John 15:7	If ye abide in me, and my words abide in you, ye shall ask what ye will, and it shall be done unto you.
John 15:8	Herein is my Father glorified, that ye bear much fruit; so shall ye be my disciples.
John 15:9	As the Father hath loved me, so have I loved you: continue ye in my love.
John 15:10	If ye keep my commandments, ye shall abide in my love; even as I have kept my Father's commandments, and abide in his love.
John 15:11	These things have I spoken unto you, that my joy might remain in you, and that your joy might be full.
John 15:12	This is my commandment, That ye love one another, as I have loved you.
John 15:13	Greater love hath no man than this, that a man lay down his life for his friends.
John 15:14	Ye are my friends, if ye do whatsoever I command you.
John 15:15a **John 15:15b**	Henceforth I call you not servants; for the servant knoweth not what his lord doeth: but I have called you friends; for all things that I have heard of my Father I have made known unto you.
John 15:16a **John 15:16b**	Ye have not chosen me, but I have chosen you, and ordained you, that ye should go and bring forth fruit, and that your fruit should remain: that whatsoever ye shall ask of the Father in my name, he may give it you.
John 15:17	These things I command you, that ye love one another.
John 15:18	If the world hate you, ye know that it hated me before it hated you.
John 15:19a **John 15:19b**	If ye were of the world, the world would love his own: but because ye are not of the world, but I have chosen you out of the world, therefore the world hateth you.
John 15:20 **John 15:20b**	Remember the word that I said unto you, The servant is not greater than his lord. If they have persecuted me, they will also persecute you; if they have kept my saying, they will keep yours also.

John 15:21	But all these things will they do unto you for my name's sake, because they know not him that sent me.
John 15:22	If I had not come and spoken unto them, they had not had sin: but now they have no cloke for their sin.
John 15:23	He that hateth me hateth my Father also.
John 15:24a **John 15:24b**	If I had not done among them the works which none other man did, they had not had sin: but now have they both seen and hated both me and my Father.
John 15:25a	But this cometh to pass, that the word might be fulfilled that is written in their law,
John 15:25b **Psalms 69:4a**	They hated me without a cause. They that hate me without a cause are more than the hairs of mine head
John 15:26a **John 15:26b**	But when the Comforter is come, whom I will send unto you from the Father, even the Spirit of truth, which proceedeth from the Father, he shall testify of me:
John 15:27	And ye also shall bear witness, because ye have been with me from the beginning.

51. I Have Overcome the World

John 16:1–33

John 16:1	These things have I spoken unto you, that ye should not be offended.
John 16:2	They shall put you out of the synagogues: yea, the time cometh, that whosoever killeth you will think that he doeth God service.
John 16:3	And these things will they do unto you, because they have not known the Father, nor me.
John 16:4a **John 16:4b**	But these things have I told you, that when the time shall come, ye may remember that I told you of them. And these things I said not unto you at the beginning, because I was with you.
John 16:5	But now I go my way to him that sent me; and none of you asketh me, Whither goest thou?
John 16:6	But because I have said these things unto you, sorrow hath filled your heart.
John 16:7a	Nevertheless I tell you the truth; It is expedient for you that I go away: for if I go not away, the Comforter will not come unto you;

John 16:7b	but if I depart, I will send him unto you.
John 16:8	And when he is come, he will reprove the world of sin, and of righteousness, and of judgment:
John 16:9	Of sin, because they believe not on me;
John 16:10	Of righteousness, because I go to my Father, and ye see me no more;
John 16:11	Of judgment, because the prince of this world is judged.
John 16:12	I have yet many things to say unto you, but ye cannot bear them now.
John 16:13a **John 16:13b**	Howbeit when he, the Spirit of truth, is come, he will guide you into all truth: for he shall not speak of himself; but whatsoever he shall hear, that shall he speak: and he will shew you things to come.
John 16:14	He shall glorify me: for he shall receive of mine, and shall shew it unto you.
John 16:15	All things that the Father hath are mine: therefore said I, that he shall take of mine, and shall shew it unto you.
John 16:16	A little while, and ye shall not see me: and again, a little while, and ye shall see me, because I go to the Father.
John 16:17a **John 16:17b**	Then said some of his disciples among themselves, What is this that he saith unto us, A little while, and ye shall not see me: and again, a little while, and ye shall see me: and, Because I go to the Father?
John 16:18	They said therefore, What is this that he saith, A little while? we cannot tell what he saith.
John 16:16a **John 16:16b**	Now Jesus knew that they were desirous to ask him, and said unto them, Do ye enquire among yourselves of that I said, A little while, and ye shall not see me: and again, a little while, and ye shall see me?
John 16:20a **John 16:20b**	Verily, verily, I say unto you, That ye shall weep and lament, but the world shall rejoice: and ye shall be sorrowful, but your sorrow shall be turned into joy.
John 16:21a **John 16:21b**	A woman when she is in travail hath sorrow, because her hour is come: but as soon as she is delivered of the child, she remembereth no more the anguish, for joy that a man is born into the world.
John 16:22	And ye now therefore have sorrow: but I will see you again, and your heart shall rejoice, and your joy no man taketh from you.
John 16:23	And in that day ye shall ask me nothing. Verily, verily, I say unto you, Whatsoever ye shall ask the Father in my name, he will give it you.

John 16:24	Hitherto have ye asked nothing in my name: ask, and ye shall receive, that your joy may be full.
John 16:25a **John 16:25b**	These things have I spoken unto you in proverbs: but the time cometh, when I shall no more speak unto you in proverbs, but I shall shew you plainly of the Father.
John 16:26	At that day ye shall ask in my name: and I say not unto you, that I will pray the Father for you:
John 16:27	For the Father himself loveth you, because ye have loved me, and have believed that I came out from God.
John 16:28	I came forth from the Father, and am come into the world: again, I leave the world, and go to the Father.
John 16:29	His disciples said unto him, Lo, now speakest thou plainly, and speakest no proverb.
John 16:30	Now are we sure that thou knowest all things, and needest not that any man should ask thee: by this we believe that thou camest forth from God.
John 16:31	Jesus answered them, Do ye now believe?
John 16:32a **John 16:32b**	Behold, the hour cometh, yea, is now come, that ye shall be scattered, every man to his own, and shall leave me alone: and yet I am not alone, because the Father is with me.
John 16:33a **John 16:33b**	These things I have spoken unto you, that in me ye might have peace. In the world ye shall have tribulation: but be of good cheer; I have overcome the world.

52. That They May Be One Even as We Are One
John 17:1–26

John 17:1	These words spake Jesus, and lifted up his eyes to heaven, and said, Father, the hour is come; glorify thy Son, that thy Son also may glorify thee:
John 17:2	As thou hast given him power over all flesh, that he should give eternal life to as many as thou hast given him.
John 17:3	And this is life eternal, that they might know thee the only true God, and Jesus Christ, whom thou hast sent.
John 17:4	I have glorified thee on the earth: I have finished the work which thou gavest me to do.
John 17:5	And now, O Father, glorify thou me with thine own self with the glory which I had with thee before the world was.

82

John 17:6a **John 17:6b**	I have manifested thy name unto the men which thou gavest me out of the world: thine they were, and thou gavest them me; and they have kept thy word.
John 17:7	Now they have known that all things whatsoever thou hast given me are of thee.
John 17:8a **John 17:8b**	For I have given unto them the words which thou gavest me; and they have received them, and have known surely that I came out from thee, and they have believed that thou didst send me.
John 17:9	I pray for them: I pray not for the world, but for them which thou hast given me; for they are thine.
John 17:10	And all mine are thine, and thine are mine; and I am glorified in them.
John 17:11a **John 17:11b**	And now I am no more in the world, but these are in the world, and I come to thee. Holy Father, keep through thine own name those whom thou hast given me, that they may be one, as we are.
John 17:12a **John 17:12b**	While I was with them in the world, I kept them in thy name: those that thou gavest me I have kept, and none of them is lost, but the son of perdition; that the scripture might be fulfilled.
John 17:13	And now come I to thee; and these things I speak in the world, that they might have my joy fulfilled in themselves.
John 17:14	I have given them thy word; and the world hath hated them, because they are not of the world, even as I am not of the world.
John 17:15	I pray not that thou shouldest take them out of the world, but that thou shouldest keep them from the evil.
John 17:16	They are not of the world, even as I am not of the world.
John 17:17	Sanctify them through thy truth: thy word is truth.
John 17:18	As thou hast sent me into the world, even so have I also sent them into the world.
John 17:19	And for their sakes I sanctify myself, that they also might be sanctified through the truth.
John 17:20	Neither pray I for these alone, but for them also which shall believe on me through their word;
John 17:21	That they all may be one; as thou, Father, art in me, and I in thee, that they also may be one in us: that the world may believe that thou hast sent me.
John 17:22	And the glory which thou gavest me I have given them; that they may be one, even as we are one:

John 17:23a	I in them, and thou in me, that they may be made perfect in one; and that the world may know that thou hast sent me, and hast loved them,
John 17:23b	as thou hast loved me.
John 17:24a	Father, I will that they also, whom thou hast given me, be with me where I am; that they may behold my glory, which thou hast given me:
John 17:24b	for thou lovedst me before the foundation of the world.
John 17:25	O righteous Father, the world hath not known thee: but I have known thee, and these have known that thou hast sent me.
John 17:26	And I have declared unto them thy name, and will declare it: that the love wherewith thou hast loved me may be in them, and I in them.

53. A Place Called Gethsemane

Matt. 26:36–46; Mark 14:32–42; Luke 22:40–46; John 18:1

Matt. 26:36a	Then cometh Jesus with them
Mark 14:32a	And came [they]
John 18:1a	When Jesus had spoken these words, he went forth with his disciples over the brook Cedron
Matt. 26:36b	unto a place called Gethsemane,
Mark 14:32b	to a place which was named Gethsemane:
John 18:1b	where was a garden, into the which he entered,
Matt. 26:36c	and saith unto the disciples, Sit ye here, while I go and pray yonder.
Mark 14:32c	and he saith to his disciples, Sit ye here, while I shall pray.
John 18:1c	and his disciples
Luke 22:40	And when he was at the place, he said unto them, Pray that ye enter not into temptation.
Matt. 26:37	And he took with him Peter and the two sons of Zebedee, and began to be sorrowful and very heavy.
Mark 14:33	And he taketh with him Peter and James and John, and began to be sore amazed, and to be very heavy;
Matt. 26:38	Then saith he unto them, My soul is exceeding sorrowful, even unto death: tarry ye here, and watch with me.
Mark 14:34	And saith unto them, My soul is exceeding sorrowful unto death: tarry ye here, and watch.
Matt. 26:39a	And he went a little further, and fell on his face, and prayed,
Mark 14:35a	And he went forward a little, and fell on the ground, and prayed
Luke 22:41a	And he was withdrawn from them about a stone's cast, and kneeled down, and prayed,

Mark 14:35b	that, if it were possible, the hour might pass from him.
Matt. 26:39b	saying, O my Father, if it be possible, let this cup pass from me:
Mark 14:36a	And he said, Abba, Father, all things are possible unto thee; take away this cup from me:
Luke 22:42a	Saying, Father, if thou be willing, remove this cup from me:
Matt. 26:39c	nevertheless not as I will, but as thou wilt.
Mark 14:36b	nevertheless not what I will, but what thou wilt.
Luke 22:42b	nevertheless not my will, but thine, be done.
Luke 22:43	And there appeared an angel unto him from heaven, strengthening him.
Luke 22:44	And being in an agony he prayed more earnestly: and his sweat was as it were great drops of blood falling down to the ground.
Matt. 26:40a	And he cometh unto the disciples, and findeth them asleep,
Mark 14:37a	And he cometh, and findeth them sleeping,
Luke 22:45	And when he rose up from prayer, and was come to his disciples, he found them sleeping for sorrow,
Matt. 26:40b	and saith unto Peter, What, could ye not watch with me one hour?
Mark 14:37b	and saith unto Peter, Simon, sleepest thou? couldest not thou watch one hour?
Luke 22:46a	And said unto them, Why sleep ye?
Matt. 26:41a	Watch and pray, that ye enter not into temptation: the spirit indeed is willing, but the flesh is weak.
Mark 14:38a	Watch ye and pray, lest ye enter into temptation. The spirit truly is ready, but the flesh is weak.
Luke 22:46b	rise and pray, lest ye enter into temptation.
Matt. 26:42a	He went away again the second time, and prayed, saying,
Mark 14:39	And again he went away, and prayed, and spake the same words.
Matt. 26:42b	O my Father, if this cup may not pass away from me, except I drink it, thy will be done.
Matt. 26:43	And he came and found them asleep again: for their eyes were heavy.
Mark 14:40	And when he returned, he found them asleep again, (for their eyes were heavy,) neither wist they what to answer him.
Matt. 26:44	And he left them, and went away again, and prayed the third time, saying the same words.
Matt. 26:45a	Then cometh he to his disciples, and saith unto them, Sleep on now, and take your rest:
Mark 14:41a	And he cometh the third time, and saith unto them, Sleep on now, and take your rest:

85

Matt. 26:45b	behold,	the hour is at hand, and	the Son of man is betrayed into the hands of sinners.
Mark 14:41b	[behold,] it is enough,	the hour is come; †	the Son of man is betrayed into the hands of sinners.
Matt. 26:46	Rise,	let us be going: behold, he is at hand	that doth betray me.
Mark 14:42	Rise up,	let us go; lo, he [is at hand]	that betrayeth me†.

PART 6

The Sixth Day of the Week

Friday

54. Betrayest Thou the Son of Man with a Kiss?

Matt. 26:47–50; Mark 14:43–45; Luke 22:47–48; John 18:2–3

John 18:2   And Judas also, which betrayed him, knew the place: for Jesus ofttimes resorted thither with his disciples.

Matt. 26:47a   And   while he yet spake, lo,   [came,]   Judas, one of the twelve,†
Mark 14:43a   And immediately,   while he yet spake,   cometh   Judas, one of the twelve,
Luke 22:47a   And   while he yet spake, behold†   [went before them,]   he that was called   Judas, one of the twelve,†
John 18:3a   And   [cometh thither]   Judas

Matt. 26:47b   and with him   a great   multitude   with swords and staves,
Mark 14:43b   and with him   a great   multitude   with swords and staves,
Luke 22:47b   [a   multitude]
John 18:3a   then,   having received   a   band of men and officers   [with lanterns and torches and weapons]

Matt. 26:47c   from the chief priests and   elders of the people.
Mark 14:43c   from the chief priests and the scribes   and the   elders.
John 18:3b   from the chief priests   and Pharisees,†‡

Luke 22:47c   and drew near unto Jesus to kiss him.

Matt. 26:48   Now he that betrayed him   gave   them a sign,   saying, Whomsoever I shall kiss, that same is he: hold   him fast.
Mark 14:44a   And he that betrayed him had   given   them a token,   saying, Whomsoever I shall kiss, that same is he; take   him,

Mark 14:44b   and lead him away safely.

Matt. 26:49   And†   he came [forthwith]   to Jesus,   and said,   Hail,   master;   and kissed him.
Mark 14:45   And as soon as he was come,   he goeth straightway   to him,   and saith,   Master, master;   and kissed him.

Matt. 26:50   And   Jesus said unto him,   Friend, wherefore art thou come?
Luke 22:48   But   Jesus said unto him, Judas,   betrayest thou the Son of man with a kiss?

55. Whom Seek Ye?

John 17:12b; 18:4–9

John 18:4 Jesus therefore, knowing all things that should come upon him, went forth, and said unto them, Whom seek ye?

John 18:5 They answered him, Jesus of Nazareth. Jesus saith unto them, I am he. And Judas also, which betrayed him, stood with them.

John 18:6 As soon then as he had said unto them, I am he, they went backward, and fell to the ground.

John 18:7 Then asked he them again, Whom seek ye? And they said, Jesus of Nazareth.

John 18:8 Jesus answered, I have told you that I am he: if therefore ye seek me, let these go their way:

John 18:9 That the saying might be fulfilled, which he spake, Of them which thou gavest me have I lost none.

John 17:12b those that thou gavest me I have kept, and none of them is lost

56. All They That Take the Sword Shall Perish with the Sword

Matt. 26:51–55; Mark 14:47–49; Luke 22:49–53; John 18:10–11

Luke 22:49 When they which were about him saw what would follow, they said unto him, Lord, shall we smite with the sword?

Matt. 26:51a And, behold, one of them which were with Jesus stretched out his hand, and drew his sword,

Mark 14:47a And one of them that stood by drew a sword,

Luke 22:50a ¶ And one of them

John 18:10a Then Simon Peter having a sword drew it,

Matt. 26:51b and struck a servant of the high priest's, and smote off his ear.

Mark 14:47b and smote a servant of the high priest, and cut off his ear.

Luke 22:50b smote the servant of the high priest, and cut off his right ear.

John 18:10b and smote the high priest's servant, and cut off his right ear. The servant's name was Malchus.

Luke 22:51 And Jesus answered and said, Suffer ye thus far. And he touched his ear, and healed him.

Matt. 26:52 Then said Jesus unto him, Put up again thy sword into his place: for all they that take the sword shall perish with the sword.

John 18:11a Then said Jesus unto Peter, Put up thy sword into the sheath:

Matt. 26:52	Thinkest thou that I cannot now pray to my Father, and he shall presently give me more than twelve legions of angels?
Matt. 26:54	But how then shall the scriptures be fulfilled, that thus it must be?
Mark 14:49b	but the scriptures must be fulfilled.
John 18:11b	the cup which my Father hath given me, shall I not drink it?
Matt. 26:55a	In that same hour said Jesus to the multitudes,
Mark 14:48a	And Jesus answered and said unto them,
Luke 22:52a	Then Jesus said unto the chief priests, and captains of the temple, and the elders,
Luke 22:52b	which were come to him,
Matt. 26:55b	Are ye come out as against a thief with swords and staves for to take me?
Mark 14:48b	Are ye come out, as against a thief, with swords and with staves to take me?
Luke 22:51a	Be ye come out, as against a thief, with swords and staves?
Matt. 26:55c	I sat daily with you teaching in the temple, and ye laid no hold on me.
Mark 14:49a	I was daily with you [teaching] in the temple†, and ye took me not:
Luke 22:53a	When I was daily with you in the temple, ye stretched forth no hands against me: but this is your hour,
Luke 22:53b	and the power of darkness.

57. All the Disciples Forsook Him

Matt. 26:50b,56; Mark 14:46,50–52; John 18:12

Matt. 26:50b	Then came they, and laid hands on Jesus, and took him.
Mark 14:46	¶ And they laid their hands on him, and took him.
John 18:12	Then the band and the captain and officers of the Jews took Jesus, and bound him,
Matt. 26:56	But all this was done, that the scriptures of the prophets might be fulfilled. Then all the disciples forsook him, and fled.
Mark 14:50	And they all forsook him, and fled.
Mark 14:51	And there followed him a certain young man, having a linen cloth cast about his naked body; and the young men laid hold on him:
Mark 14:52	And he left the linen cloth, and fled from them naked.

58. Into the High Priest's House

Matt. 26:57–58; Mark 14:53–54; Luke 22:54–55; John 11:50b; 18:13–18

Matt. 26:57a	¶ And they that had laid hold on Jesus led him away
Mark 14:53a	¶ And they led Jesus away
Luke 22:54a	¶ Then took they him, and led him, and brought him
John 18:13a	And led him away to Annas first;
Matt. 26:57b	to Caiaphas the high priest,
Mark 14:53b	to the high priest:
Luke 22:54a	into the high priest's house.
John 18:13b	to Caiaphas, which was the high priest that same year.
	for he was father in law
Matt. 26:57c	and with him where [were assembled] ‡ and the elders † [the scribes].
Mark 14:53c	were assembled all the chief priests and the elders and the scribes.
John 18:14	Now Caiaphas was he, which gave counsel to the Jews, that it was expedient that one man should die for the people.
John 11:50b	that it is expedient for us, that one man should die for the people,
Matt. 26:58a	But Peter followed him afar off
Mark 14:54a	And Peter followed him afar off,
Luke 22:54b	And Peter followed afar off.
John 18:15a	¶ And Simon Peter followed Jesus, and so did another disciple: that disciple was known unto the high priest,
Matt. 26:58b	unto the high priest's palace,
Mark 14:54b	even into the palace of the high priest:
John 18:15b	into the palace of the high priest.
	and went in with Jesus
John 19:16a	But Peter stood at the door without. Then went out that other disciple, which was known unto the high priest,
John 19:16b	and spake unto her that kept the door, and brought in Peter.
Matt. 26:58b	and went in, and sat with the servants, to see the end.
Mark 14:54b	and he sat with the servants,
Luke 22:55a	[Peter sat down among them]
John 18:18a	the servants and officers stood there,
Luke 22:55b	when they had kindled a fire in the midst of the hall, and were set down together, †:
John 18:18b	who had made a fire of coals; for it was cold: and they warmed themselves:

92

Mark 14:54c	and warmed himself at the fire.
John 18:18c	and Peter stood with them, and warmed himself.

59. Art Thou the Christ, the Son of the Blessed?

Matt. 26:59–66; Mark 14:55–64

Matt. 26:59	Now the chief priests, and elders, and all the council, sought false witness against Jesus, to put him to death;
Mark 14:55a	And the chief priests and all the council sought for witness against Jesus to put him to death;
Matt. 26:60a	But found none: yea, though many false witnesses came, yet found they none.
Mark 14:55b	And found none.
Mark 14:56	For many bare false witness against him, but their witness agreed not together.
Matt. 26:60b	At the last came two false witnesses,
Mark 14:57	And there arose certain, and bare false witness against him, saying,
Matt. 26:61a	And said, This fellow said, I am able to destroy the temple of God,
Mark 14:58a	We heard him say, I will destroy this temple that is made with hands,
Matt. 26:61b	and [in three days] to build it].
Mark 14:58b	and within three days I will build another made without hands.
Mark 14:59	But neither so did their witness agree together.
Matt. 26:62	And the high priest arose, and said unto him, Answerest thou nothing? what is it which these witness against thee?
Mark 14:60	And the high priest stood up in the midst, and asked Jesus, saying, Answerest thou nothing? what is it which these witness against thee?
Matt. 26:63a	But Jesus held his peace. And the high priest answered and said unto him,
Mark 14:61a	But he held his peace, and answered nothing. Again the high priest asked him, and said unto him,
Matt. 26:63b	I adjure thee by the living God, that thou tell us whether thou be the Christ, the Son of God.
Mark 14:61b	Art thou the Christ, the Son of the Blessed?
Matt. 26:64a	Jesus saith unto him, Thou hast said: nevertheless I say unto you,
Mark 14:62a	And Jesus said, I am:

Matt. 26:64b	Hereafter [ye] shall †	see the Son of man sitting on the right hand of power, and coming in the clouds of heaven.
Mark 14:62b	and ye shall	see the Son of man sitting on the right hand of power, and coming in the clouds of heaven.

Matt. 26:65a	Then the high priest rent his clothes, saying, He hath spoken blasphemy; what further need have we of witnesses?
Mark 14:63	Then the high priest rent his clothes, and saith, What [further] need we any † witnesses?

Matt. 26:65b	behold, now ye have heard his blasphemy.
Mark 14:64a	Ye have heard the blasphemy:

Matt. 26:66	What think ye? They answered and said, He is guilty of death.
Mark 14:64b	what think ye? And they all condemned him to be guilty of death.

60. Prophesy Unto Us, Thou Christ

Matt. 26:67–68; Mark 14:65; Luke 22:63–65

Matt. 26:67a	Then did they spit in
Mark 14:65a	And some began to spit on him,
Luke 22:63a	¶ And the men that held Jesus mocked him, and

Matt. 26:67b	his face, and buffeted him;
Mark 14:65b	and to cover his face, and to buffet him,
Luke 22:64a	And when they had blindfolded him, they struck him on the face,

Matt. 26:67b	and others smote him with the palms of their hands,
Mark 14:65c	and the servants did strike him with the palms of their hands.
Luke 22:63b	smote him

Matt. 26:68	Saying, Prophesy unto us, thou Christ, Who is he that smote thee?
Mark 14:65b	and to say unto him, Prophesy:
Luke 22:64b	saying, Prophesy, who is it that smote thee?

Luke 22:65	And many other things blasphemously spake they against him.

61. Thou Also Wast with Jesus with Jesus of Nazareth

Matt. 26:69–75; Mark 14:66–72; Luke 22:56–62; John 18:17,25–27

Matt. 26:69a	¶Now	Peter sat without	in the palace: and	there †	a		damsel	
Mark 14:66a	¶And as	Peter was beneath	in the palace,	†	one of	the	maids	of the high priest
Luke 22:56a	But				a certain	the	maid	
John 18:17a	Then			†	the		damsel	that kept the door unto

Matt. 26:69b	came	unto	him,
Mark 14:66b	[cometh]:		
Luke 22:56b	beheld		him

Matt. 26:69c				saying,
Mark 14:67a	And when she saw	Peter	warming himself,	she	looked upon him, and	said,
Luke 22:56c	as	he	sat by the fire,	and	earnestly looked upon him, and	said,
John 18:17b						[saith]

Matt. 26:69d	Thou	also wast	with	Jesus of Galilee.
Mark 14:67b	thou	also wast	with	Jesus of Nazareth.
Luke 22:56c	This man	was also	with	him.
John 18:17c	Art not thou also one of this man's disciples?

Matt. 26:70	But	he denied	before them all,	saying,	I know	not	what thou sayest.
Mark 14:68a	But	he denied,		saying,	I know	not, neither understand I	what thou sayest.
Luke 22:57	And	he denied him,		saying, Woman,	I know him	not.
John 18:17d		He		saith,	I am	not.

Matt. 26:71a	And when	he	was gone	out into the porch,	
Mark 14:68b	And	he	went	out into the porch;	and the cock crew.
John 18:25a	And	Simon Peter			stood and warmed himself.

Matt. 26:71b		another maid	saw him,
Mark 14:69a	And	a maid	saw him again.
Luke 22:58a	And after a little while	another	saw him,

Matt. 26:71c	and	said	unto	them that were there,	This fellow	was	also		with Jesus of Nazareth.
Mark 14:69b	and	began to say	to	them that stood by,	This	is		one	of them.
Luke 22:58b	and	said,			Thou	art	also		of them.

95

John 18:25b	They said therefore unto him, Art not thou also one of his disciples?
Matt. 26:72	And again he denied with an oath, I do not know the man.
Mark 14:70a	And he denied it again.
Luke 22:58c	And Peter said, Man, I am not.
John 18:25c	He denied it, and said, I am not.
Matt. 26:73a	And after a while came unto him they that stood by,
Mark 14:70b	And a little after, they that stood by
Luke 22:59a	And about the space of one hour after another confidently affirmed,
John 18:26a	One of the servants of the high priest, being his kinsman whose ear Peter cut off,
Matt. 26:73b	and said to Peter,
Mark 14:70c	said again to Peter,
Luke 22:59b	saying,
John 18:26b	saith,
Matt. 26:73c	Surely thou also art one of them;
Mark 14:70d	Surely thou art one of them:
Luke 22:59c	Of a truth this fellow also was with him:
John 18:26c	Did not I see thee in the garden with him?
Matt. 26:73d	for thy speech bewrayeth thee.
Mark 14:70e	for thou art a Galilaean, and thy speech agreeth thereto.
Luke 22:59d	for he is a Galilaean.
Matt. 26:74a	Then [he] began † to curse and to swear, saying, I know not the man.
Mark 14:71a	But he began to curse and to swear, saying, I know not this man of whom ye speak.
Luke 22:60a	And Peter said, Man, I know not what thou sayest.
John 18:27a	Peter then denied again:
Matt. 26:74b	And immediately the cock crew.
Mark 14:72a	And the second time the cock crew.
Luke 22:60b	And immediately, while he yet spake, the cock crew.
John 18:27b	and immediately the cock crew.
Luke 22:61a	And the Lord turned, and looked upon Peter.

Matt. 26:75a	And Peter remembered	the word of	Jesus,	which		said unto him,	Before the cock crow,	thou shalt deny me thrice.
Mark 14:72b	And Peter called to mind	the word that	Jesus			said unto him,	Before the cock crow twice,	thou shalt deny me thrice.
Luke 22:61b	And Peter remembered	the word of the	Lord, how	he	had	said unto him,	Before the cock crow,	thou shalt deny me thrice.

Matt. 26:75b	And		he	went out, and wept bitterly.
Mark 14:72c	And when he thought thereon,		he	wept.
Luke 22:62	And		Peter	went out, and wept bitterly.

62. When the Morning Was Come

Matt. 27:1; Mark 15:1; Luke 22:66–71

Matt. 27:1a		When		the morning was come
Mark 15:1a	And		straightway in	the morning
Luke 22:66a	¶ And as soon as it was day,			

Matt. 27:1b	all	the chief priests	and		elders of the people	and	scribes]
Mark 15:1b		the chief priests		[with	the	elders	and the †‡ scribes
Luke 22:66b		the [chief priests]	[and		the] elders of the people		

Matt. 27:1c	took counsel	against Jesus to put him to death:		
Mark 15:1c	held a consultation †			the whole council,
Luke 22:66c	came together,	and		council, saying,
		and led him into their		

Luke 22:67   Art thou the Christ? tell us. And he said unto them, If I tell you, ye will not believe:

Luke 22:68   And if I also ask you, ye will not answer me, nor let me go.

Luke 22:69   Hereafter shall the Son of man sit on the right hand of the power of God.

Luke 22:70   Then said they all, Art thou then the Son of God? And he said unto them, Ye say that I am.

Luke 22:71   And they said, What need we any further witness? for we ourselves have heard of his own mouth.

63. I Have Betrayed the Innocent Blood

Matt. 27:3–10; Zech. 11:12–13

Matt. 27:3a	¶ Then Judas, which had betrayed him, when he saw that he was condemned, repented himself, and brought again the thirty pieces of
Matt. 27:3b	silver to the chief priests and elders,
Matt. 27:4	Saying, I have sinned in that I have betrayed the innocent blood. And they said, What is that to us? see thou to that.
Matt. 27:5	And he cast down the pieces of silver in the temple, and departed, and went and hanged himself.
Matt. 27:6	And the chief priests took the silver pieces, and said, It is not lawful for to put them into the treasury, because it is the price of blood.
Matt. 27:7	And they took counsel, and bought with them the potter's field, to bury strangers in.
Matt. 27:8	Wherefore that field was called, The field of blood, unto this day.
Matt. 27:9a	Then was fulfilled that which was spoken by Jeremy the prophet, saying,
Matt. 27:9b / **Zech. 11:12b**	And they took the thirty pieces of silver, the price of him that was valued, † thirty pieces of silver. [So they weighed for my price]
Matt. 27:9c	whom they of the children of Israel did value;
Matt. 27:10 / **Zech. 11:13b**	And gave them for the potter's field, as the Lord appointed me. and cast them to the potter in the house of the LORD.

64. When Herod Saw Jesus

Luke 23:8–12

Luke 23:8a	¶ And when Herod saw Jesus, he was exceeding glad: for he was desirous to see him of a long season, because he had heard many things of him;
Luke 23:8b	and he hoped to have seen some miracle done by him.
Luke 23:9	Then he questioned with him in many words; but he answered him nothing.
Luke 23:10	And the chief priests and scribes stood and vehemently accused him.
Luke 23:11	And Herod with his men of war set him at nought, and mocked him, and arrayed him in a gorgeous robe, and sent him again to Pilate.

Luke 23:12 ¶ And the same day Pilate and Herod were made friends together: for before they were at enmity between themselves.

65. A Notable Prisoner Called Barabbas

Matt. 27:15–23; Mark 15:6–14; Luke 23:13–23; John 18:39–40

Luke 23:13 ¶ And Pilate, when he had called together the chief priests and the rulers and the people,

Luke 23:14a Said unto them, Ye have brought this man unto me, as one that perverteth the people: and, behold, I, having examined him before you,
Luke 23:14b have found no fault in this man touching those things whereof ye accuse him:

Luke 23:15 No, nor yet Herod: for I sent you to him; and, lo, nothing worthy of death is done unto him.

Luke 23:16 I will therefore chastise him, and release him.

Matt. 27:15a	Now at that feast	[was wont to]	the governor †	release	unto the people a prisoner,
Mark 15:6a	Now at that feast		he	released	unto them one prisoner,
Luke 23:17	[For [at the feast]	of necessity	he must	release‡	unto them†: [one]
John 18:39a	But [at the passover]		I should	release	unto you one†:

Matt. 27:15b	whom	they would.
Mark 15:6b	whomsoever	they desired.

Matt. 27:16 And they had then a notable prisoner, called Barabbas.
Mark 15:7a And there was one named Barabbas, which lay bound with them that had made insurrection with him,

Mark 15:7b who had committed murder in the insurrection.

Mark 15:8 And the multitude crying aloud began to desire him to do as he had ever done unto them.

Matt. 27:17a Therefore when they were gathered together, Pilate said unto them, Whom will ye that I release unto you?
Mark 15:9a But Pilate answered them, saying, Will ye that I release unto you
John 18:39b ye therefore that I release unto you

Matt. 21:17b Barabbas, or Jesus which is called Christ?
Mark 15:9b the King of the Jews?
John 18:39b the King of the Jews?

Matt. 21:18 For he knew that for envy they had delivered him.
Mark 15:10 For he knew that [for envy] the chief priests had delivered him†.

Matt. 27:19a ¶ When he was set down on the judgment seat, his wife sent unto him, saying, Have thou nothing to do with that just man:
Matt. 27:19b for I have suffered many things this day in a dream because of him.

Matt. 27:20 But the chief priests and elders persuaded the multitude that they should ask Barabbas, and destroy Jesus.
Mark 15:11 But the chief priests moved the people, that he should rather release Barabbas unto them.

Matt. 27:21a The governor answered and said unto them, Whether of the twain will ye that I release unto you?

Matt. 27:21b They said, Barabbas.
Luke 23:18 And they cried out all at once, saying, Away with this man, and release unto us Barabbas:
John 18:40 Then cried they all again, saying, Not this man, but Barabbas. Now Barabbas was a robber.

Luke 23:19 (Who for a certain sedition made in the city, and for murder, was cast into prison.)

Matt. 27:22a Pilate saith unto them,
Mark 15:12a And Pilate answered and said again unto them,
Luke 23:20a Pilate therefore, willing to release Jesus, spake again to them.

Matt. 27:22b What shall I do then with Jesus which is called Christ?
Mark 15:12b What will ye then that I shall do unto him whom ye call the King of the Jews?

Matt. 27:22c They all say unto him, Let him be crucified.
Mark 15:13 And they cried out again, Crucify him.
Luke 23:21 But they cried, saying, Crucify him, crucify him.

Matt. 27:23a And the governor said, Why, what evil hath he done?
Mark 15:14a Then Pilate said unto them, Why, what evil hath he done?
Luke 23:22a And he said unto them the third time, Why, what evil hath he done? I have found no cause of death in him:

Luke 23:22b I will therefore chastise him, and let him go.

Matt. 27:23b But they cried out the more, saying, Let him be crucified.
Mark 15:14b And they cried out the more exceedingly, Crucify him.
Luke 23:23a And they were instant with loud voices, requiring that he might be crucified.

Luke 23:23b   And the voices of them and of the chief priests prevailed.

66. Into the Hall, Called Praetorium

Matt. 27:27–30; Mark 15:16–19; John 19:1–3

John 19:1	Then Pilate therefore took Jesus, and scourged him.
Matt. 27:27a	Then the soldiers of the governor took Jesus into the common hall,
Mark 15:16a	And the soldiers led him away into the hall, called Praetorium;
Matt. 27:27b	and gathered unto him the whole band of soldiers.
Mark 15:16b	and they call together the whole band.
Matt. 27:28	And they stripped him, and put on him a scarlet robe.
Mark 15:17a	And they clothed him with purple,
John 19:2b	and they put on him a purple robe,
Matt. 27:29a	And when they had platted a crown of thorns, they put it upon his head,
Mark 15:17b	and platted a crown of thorns, and put it about his head,
John 19:2a	And the soldiers platted a crown of thorns, put it on his head,
Matt. 27:29b	and a reed in his right hand: and they bowed the knee before him,
Mark 15:17c	and bowing their knees worshipped him.
Matt. 27:29c	and mocked him, saying, Hail, King of the Jews!
Mark 15:18	And began to salute him, Hail, King of the Jews!
John 19:3a	And said, Hail, King of the Jews!
Matt. 27:30	And they spit on him, and took the reed, and smote him on the head.
Mark 15:19a	†[and did spit upon him,] ‡[with a reed] And they smote him on the head ‡,†
John 19:3b	And they smote him with their hands.

67. Behold the Man!

John 19:4–15

John 19:4   Pilate therefore went forth again, and saith unto them, Behold, I bring him forth to you, that ye may know that I find no fault in him.

John 19:5   Then came Jesus forth, wearing the crown of thorns, and the purple robe. And Pilate saith unto them, Behold the man!

John 19:6a   When the chief priests therefore and officers saw him, they cried out, saying, Crucify him, crucify him. Pilate saith unto them,
John 19:6b   Take ye him, and crucify him: for I find no fault in him.

John 19:7   The Jews answered him, We have a law, and by our law he ought to die, because he made himself the Son of God.

John 19:8   ¶ When Pilate therefore heard that saying, he was the more afraid;

John 19:9   And went again into the judgment hall, and saith unto Jesus, Whence art thou? But Jesus gave him no answer.

John 19:10   Then saith Pilate unto him, Speakest thou not unto me? knowest thou not that I have power to crucify thee, and have power to release thee?

John 19:11a   Jesus answered, Thou couldest have no power at all against me, except it were given thee from above: therefore he that delivered me
John 19:11b   unto thee hath the greater sin.

John 19:12a   And from thenceforth Pilate sought to release him: but the Jews cried out, saying, If thou let this man go, thou art not Caesar's friend:
John 19:12b   whosoever maketh himself a king speaketh against Caesar.

John 19:13a   ¶ When Pilate therefore heard that saying, he brought Jesus forth, and sat down in the judgment seat in a place that is called the Pavement,
John 19:13b   but in the Hebrew, Gabbatha.

John 19:14   And it was the preparation of the passover, and about the sixth hour: and he saith unto the Jews, Behold your King!

John 19:15a   But they cried out, Away with him, away with him, crucify him. Pilate saith unto them, Shall I crucify your King?
John 19:15b   The chief priests answered, We have no king but Caesar.

68. And Pilate Gave Sentence

Matt. 27:24–26; Mark 15:15; Luke 23:24–25; John 19:16a

Matt. 27:24a   When Pilate saw that he could prevail nothing, but that rather a tumult was made, he took water, and washed his hands before the multitude, saying,
Matt. 27:24b   I am innocent of the blood of this just person: see ye to it.

Matt. 27:25	Then answered all the people, and said, His blood be on us, and on our children.

Mark 15:15a	And	so Pilate,	willing to content the people,	
Luke 23:24	And	Pilate		gave sentence that it should be as they required.

Matt. 27:26	Then	[he]	released †	Barabbas	unto them:
Mark 15:15b	And	he	released	Barabbas	unto them,
Luke 23:25a	And	he	released	unto them	him that for sedition and murder was cast into prison, whom they desired;

Matt. 27:26b	and	when he had scourged Jesus,	he	delivered him	to be crucified.
Mark 15:15c		[when he had scourged him,]	and	delivered Jesus, †	to be crucified.
Luke 23:25b	but		he	delivered Jesus	to their will.
John 19:16a	Then		[he]	delivered † him	therefore unto them	to be crucified.

69. Simon of Cyrene

Matt. 27:31–32; Mark 15:20–21; Luke 23:26; John 19:16

Matt. 27:31a	And after that	they had mocked him, they took	the robe	off	from him,
Mark 15:20a	And when	they had mocked him, they took †	the purple	[off]	from him,

Matt. 27:31b	and put his own raiment on him,	and led him away	to crucify him.
Mark 15:20b	and put his own clothes on him,	and led him out	to crucify him.
John 19:16b	And they took Jesus,	and led him away.	

Matt. 27:32a	And as they came out,	they found	a man	[Simon] of Cyrene, † by name:		
Mark 15:21b	And †	they laid hold upon	one	Simon a	Cyrenian,	who passed by,	coming out of the country,
Luke 23:26a	And as they	led him away, they laid hold upon	one	Simon, a	Cyrenian,		coming out of the country,

Matt. 27:32c		him	they compelled	to bear	his cross.
Mark 15:21c	and on	him	[they compel]	[to bear	his cross.]
Luke 23:26b	the father of Alexander and Rufus, ‡		they	laid	the cross,	that he might bear it after Jesus.

70. Daughters of Jerusalem, Weep Not for Me
Luke 23:27–31

Luke 23:27   ¶ And there followed him a great company of people, and of women, which also bewailed and lamented him.

Luke 23:28   But Jesus turning unto them said, Daughters of Jerusalem, weep not for me, but weep for yourselves, and for your children.

Luke 23:29a   For, behold, the days are coming, in the which they shall say, Blessed are the barren, and the wombs that never bare,
Luke 23:29b   and the paps which never gave suck.

Luke 23:30   Then shall they begin to say to the mountains, Fall on us; and to the hills, Cover us.

Luke 23:31   For if they do these things in a green tree, what shall be done in the dry?

71. A Place Called Golgotha
Matt. 27:33–34; Mark 15:22; Luke 23:33; John 19:17

Matt. 27:33a	And when	they were come	unto a place	called	Golgotha,
Mark 15:22a	And	they bring him	unto the place	called	Golgotha,
Luke 23:33a	And when	they were come	to the place,	called	Calvary,
John 19:17a	And	he bearing his cross went forth	into a place	called in the Hebrew	[which is Golgotha:]

Matt. 27:33b	a place	that is to say,	of a skull,
Mark 15:22b	The place	which is, being interpreted,	of a skull.
John 19:17b	the place	called	of a skull, †

Matt. 27:34a	¶They gave him [to drink] vinegar † mingled with gall:	and when he had tasted thereof, he would not drink.
Mark 15:23a	And they gave him to drink wine mingled with myrrh:	but he received it not.

72. There They Crucified Him
Matt. 27:38; Mark 15:25,27–28 Luke 23:33b–34a; John 19:18; Isaiah 53:12b

Mark 15:25	And it was the third hour, and	they crucified him.
Luke 23:33b	there	they crucified him,
John 19:18a	Where	they crucified him,

Luke 23:24a ¶ Then said Jesus, Father, forgive them; for they know not what they do.

Matt. 27:38a Then [with him] were there two thieves crucified†,
Mark 15:27a And with him they † two thieves [crucify];
Luke 23:33a and the malefactors,
John 19:18a and [with him] two other†, on either side one,

Matt. 27:38b one on the right hand, and another on the left.
Mark 15:27b the one on his right hand, and the other on his left.
Luke 23:33b one on the right hand, and the other on the left.
John 19:18b and Jesus in the midst.

Mark 15:28 And the scripture was fulfilled, which saith, And he was numbered with the transgressors.
Isa. 53:12b and he was numbered with the transgressors;

73. The Superscription of His Accusation
Matthew 27:37; Mark 15:26; Luke 23:38; John 19:19–22

John 19:19a And Pilate wrote a title,

Matt. 27:37a And † his accusation written, [set up over his head]
Mark 15:26a And the superscription of his accusation was written over,
Luke 23:38a And a superscription also was written over him
John 19:19a and put it on the cross.

Luke 23:38b in letters of Greek, and Latin, and Hebrew,
John 19:20b and it was written †‡ Greek, and Latin. [and] [Hebrew,]

Matt. 27:37b THIS IS JESUS THE KING OF THE JEWS.
Mark 15:26b THE KING OF THE JEWS.
Luke 23:38b THIS IS THE KING OF THE JEWS.
John 19:19b JESUS OF NAZARETH THE KING OF THE JEWS.

John 19:20a This title then read many of the Jews: for the place where Jesus was crucified was nigh to the city:

John 19:21 Then said the chief priests of the Jews to Pilate, Write not, The King of the Jews; but that he said, I am King of the Jews.

John 19:22   Pilate answered, What I have written I have written.

74. They Parted My Garments Among Them

Matt. 27:35–36; Mark 15:24b–34; Luke 23:34b–34c; John 19:23–24; Psalms 22:17b–18

Matt. 27:35a	And		they	crucified him,	and	parted his garments,
Mark 15:24a	And when		they had	crucified him,	they	parted his garments,
Luke 23:34b	And		they had	crucified him,	they	parted his raiment,
John 19:23a	Then [when]	the soldiers, †	they had	crucified Jesus,	took	his garments, and made four parts, to every soldier a part;

John 19:23b   and also his coat: now the coat was without seam, woven from the top throughout.

Matt. 27:35b		casting	lots:	
Mark 15:24b		casting	lots	upon them, what every man should take.
Luke 23:34c		cast	lots.	
John 19:24a	and	cast	lots	for it, whose it shall be:

They said therefore among themselves, Let us not rend it, but

Matt. 27:35c	that it	might be fulfilled which was spoken by the prophet,	They parted my garments among them,
John 19:24b	that the scripture	might be fulfilled, which saith,	They parted my raiment among them,
Psalms 22:18a	and		They part my garments among them,

Matt. 27:35d	and	upon	my vesture	did they cast lots.
John 19:24c	and	for	my vesture	they did cast lots.
Psalms 22:18b	and	[upon	my vesture]	cast lots†.

Matt. 27:36	And sitting down	they watched him there;
Psalms 22:17b		they look and stare upon me.

John 19:24d   These things therefore the soldiers did.

75. Save Thyself and Come Down from the Cross

Matt. 27:39-43; Mark 15:29-32; Luke 23:35-37

Luke 23:35a   And the people stood beholding.

Matt. 27:39	¶ And they that passed by reviled him, wagging their heads,
Mark 15:29a	And they that passed by railed on him, wagging their heads,
Matt. 27:40a	And saying, Thou that destroyest the temple, and buildest it in three days,
Mark 15:29b	and saying, Ah, thou that destroyest the temple, and buildest it in three days,
Matt. 27:40b	save thyself. If thou be the Son of God, come down from the cross.
Mark 15:30	Save thyself, and come down from the cross.
Matt. 27:41	Likewise also the chief priests mocking him, with the scribes and elders, said,
Mark 15:31a	Likewise also the chief priests mocking [with the scribes,] said among themselves †
Luke 23:35b	And the rulers also with them derided him, saying,
Matt. 27:42a	He saved others; himself he cannot save.
Mark 15:31b	He saved others; himself he cannot save.
Luke 23:35c	He saved others; [himself] let him save†, the chosen of God.
Matt. 27:42b	If he be the King of Israel, let him now come down from the cross, and we will believe him.
Mark 15:32	Let Christ the King of Israel [now] descend † from the cross, that we may see and believe.
Luke 23:35d	if he be Christ,
Matt. 27:43	He trusted in God; let him deliver him now, if he will have him: for he said, I am the Son of God.
Luke 23:36	And the soldiers also mocked him, coming to him, and offering him vinegar,
Luke 23:37	And saying, If thou be the king of the Jews, save thyself.

76. To Day Shalt Thou Be with Me in Paradise
Matt. 27:44; Mark 15:32b; Luke 23:39–43

Matt. 27:44	The thieves also, which were crucified with him, cast the same in his teeth.
Mark 15:32b	And they that were crucified with him reviled him.
Luke 23:39a	And one of the malefactors which were hanged railed on him, saying,
Luke 23:39b	If thou be the Christ, save thyself and us.
Luke 23:40	But the other answering rebuked him, saying, Dost not thou fear God, seeing thou art in the same condemnation?

Luke 23:41 And we indeed justly; for we receive the due reward of our deeds: but this man hath done nothing amiss.

Luke 23:42 And he said unto Jesus, Lord, remember me when thou comest into thy kingdom.

Luke 23:43 And Jesus said unto him, Verily I say unto thee, To day shalt thou be with me in paradise.

77. Behold Thy Mother
John 19:25–27

John 19:25 ¶Now there stood by the cross of Jesus his mother, and his mother's sister, Mary the wife of Cleophas, and Mary Magdalene.

John 19:26 When Jesus therefore saw his mother, and the disciple standing by, whom he loved, he saith unto his mother, Woman, behold thy son!

John 19:27 Then saith he to the disciple, Behold thy mother! And from that hour that disciple took her unto his own home.

78. There Was Darkness
Matthew 27:45; Mark 15:33; Luke 23:44–45a

Matt 27:45	Now from the sixth hour	there was darkness over all the land	unto the ninth hour.
Mark 15:33	And when the sixth hour was come,	there was darkness over the whole land	until the ninth hour.
Luke 23:44	And it was about the sixth hour, and	there was darkness over all the earth	until the ninth hour.
Luke 23:45a	And	the sun was darkened,	

79. Eli, Eli, Lama Sabachthani
Matt. 27:45–49; Mark 15:33–36; Luke 23:45a; John 19:28–29; Psalms 22:1;69:21

Matt. 27:46a	And about the ninth hour Jesus cried with a loud voice, saying, Eli,	Eli, lama sabachthani? that is	to say,
Mark 15:34a	And at the ninth hour Jesus cried with a loud voice, saying, Eloi,	Eloi, lama sabachthani? which is,	being interpreted,

Matt. 27:46b My God, my God, why hast thou forsaken me?

Mark 15:34b My God, my God, why hast thou forsaken me?

Psalms 22:1a My God, my God, why hast thou forsaken me?

Matt. 27:47 Some of them that stood there, when they heard that, said, This man calleth for Elias.
Mark 15:35 And some of them that stood by, when they heard it, said, Behold, he calleth Elias.

John 19:28a After this, Jesus knowing that all things were now accomplished, that the scripture might be fulfilled, saith,

John 19:28b I thirst.
Psalms 69:21b and in my thirst they gave me

John 19:29a Now there was set a vessel full of vinegar:

Matt. 27:48a And straightway one of them ran, and took a spunge, and filled it with vinegar, and put it on a reed,
Mark 15:36a And one ran, and [a spunge] filled† full of vinegar, and put it on a reed,
John 19:29b and they [a spunge] filled† with vinegar, and put it upon hyssop, and put it to his mouth.
Psalms 69:21b vinegar

Matt. 27:48b and gave him to drink.
Mark 15:36b and gave him to drink,
Psalms 69:21c to drink.

Matt. 27:49 The rest said, Let be, let us see whether Elias will come to save him.
Mark 15:36b saying, Let alone: let us see whether Elias will come to take him down.

80. It Is Finished

Matt. 27:50–51; Mark 15:37–38; Luke 23:45b–46; John 19:30; Psalms 31:5a

John 19:30 When Jesus therefore had received the vinegar, he said, It is finished:

Matt. 27:50a [when] Jesus, † he had cried again with a loud voice, and
Mark 15:37a And Jesus cried with a loud voice,
Luke 23:46b And when Jesus had cried with a loud voice, he said, Father, into thy hands I commend my spirit: and having said thus, he
Psalms 31:5a Into thine hands I commit my spirit:

Matt. 27:50b yielded up the ghost.
Mark 15:37b gave up the ghost.
Luke 23:46b gave up the ghost.

81. The Veil of the Temple Was Rent

Matt. 27:51; Mark 15:38; Luke 23:45b

Matt. 27:51 And, behold, the veil of the temple was rent in twain from the top to the bottom; and the earth did quake, and the rocks rent;

Mark 15:38 And the veil of the temple was rent in twain from the top to the bottom.

Luke 23:45b and the veil of the temple was rent in the midst.

82. Truly This Man Was the Son of God

Matt. 27:54; Mark 15:39; Luke 23:47

Matt. 27:54a Now when the centurion,

Mark 15:39a And when the centurion, which stood over against him,

Luke 23:47a Now when the centurion

and they that were with him, watching Jesus,

Matt. 27:54b saw the earthquake, and those things that were done,

Mark 15:39b saw that he so cried out, and gave up the ghost,

they feared greatly,

Luke 23:47b saw what was done, he glorified God,

Matt. 27:54c saying, Truly this was the Son of God.

Mark 15:39c he said, Truly this man was the Son of God.

Luke 23:47c saying, Certainly, this was a righteous man.

83. With a Spear Pierced His Side

John 19:31–37; Psalms 34:20; Zech. 12:10

John 19:31a The Jews therefore, because it was the preparation, that the bodies should not remain upon the cross on the sabbath day,

John 19:31b (for that sabbath day was an high day,) besought Pilate that their legs might be broken, and that they might be taken away.

John 19:32 Then came the soldiers, and brake the legs of the first, and of the other which was crucified with him.

John 19:33 But when they came to Jesus, and saw that he was dead already, they brake not his legs:

John 19:34 But one of the soldiers with a spear pierced his side, and forthwith came there out blood and water.

John 19:35 And he that saw it bare record, and his record is true: and he knoweth that he saith true, that ye might believe.

110

John 19:36 — For these things were done, that the scripture should be fulfilled, A bone of him shall not be broken.
Psalms 34:20 — He keepeth all his bones: not one of them is broken.

John 19:37 — And again another scripture saith, They shall look on him whom they pierced.
Zech. 12:10b — they shall look upon me whom they have pierced

84. Many Women Were There Beholding Afar Off

Matt. 27:55–56; Mark 15:40–41; Luke 23:49

Matt. 27:55a — And many women were there† [beholding] afar off,
Mark 15:40a — There were also women† [looking on] afar off:
Luke 23:49a — †and the women [†And all his acquaintance,]‡ stood afar off, beholding these things.

Matt. 27:56 — Among which was Mary Magdalene, and Mary the mother of James and Joses, and the mother of Zebedee's children.
Mark 15:40b — among whom was May Magdalene, and Mary the mother of James the less and of Joses, and Salome;

Matt. 27:55b — which ministering unto him; followed Jesus from Galilee,†
Mark 15:41a — (Who also, when he was in Galilee, [†and ministered unto him;] [and] followed him;† from Galilee,]
Luke 23:49b — [‡that followed him

Mark 15:41b — and many other women which came up with him unto Jerusalem.

85. Then Took They the Body Of Jesus

Matt. 27:57–61; Mark 15:42–47; Luke 23:50–56; John 19:38–42

Matt. 27:57a — When the even was come,
Mark 15:42 — And now when the even was come, because it was the preparation, that is, the day before the sabbath,

Matt. 27:57b — there came a rich man [†named Joseph,] of Arimathaea,† an honourable
Mark 15:43a — Joseph of Arimathaea, counsellor,
Luke 23:50 — And, behold, there was a man named Joseph, a counsellor;
Luke 23:51b — of Arimathaea, a city of the Jews:
John 19:38a — And after this Joseph of Arimathaea,

Matt. 27:57c — who also himself

111

Mark 15:43b	which waited for the kingdom of God,
Luke 23:50b	and he was a good man, and a just:
Luke 23:51b	who also himself waited for the kingdom of God.
Matt. 27:57d	was Jesus' disciple:
John 19:38b	being a disciple of Jesus, but secretly for fear of the Jews,
Luke 23:51a	(The same had not consented to the counsel and deed of them;)
Matt. 27:58a	He went to Pilate, and begged the body of Jesus.
Mark 15:43b	came, and went in boldly unto Pilate, and craved the body of Jesus.
Luke 23:52	This man went unto Pilate, and begged the body of Jesus.
John 19:38c	[†Pilate] besought† that he might take away the body of Jesus:
Mark 15:44	And Pilate marvelled if he were already dead: and calling unto him the centurion, he asked him whether he had been any while dead.
Mark 15:45a	And when he knew it of the centurion,
Matt. 27:58b	Then Pilate commanded the body to be delivered.
Mark 15:45b	he gave the body to Joseph.
John 19:38c	and Pilate gave him leave. He came therefore, and took the body of Jesus.
John 19:39a	And there came also Nicodemus, which at the first came to Jesus by night, and brought a mixture of myrrh and aloes,
John 19:39b	about an hundred pound weight.
Matt. 27:59a	And when Joseph had taken the body,
Mark 15:46a	And when he bought fine linen, and took him down,
Luke 23:53a	And he took it down,
John 19:40a	Then took they the body of Jesus,
Matt. 27:59b	he wrapped it in a clean linen cloth,
Mark 15:46b	and wrapped him in the linen,
Luke 23:53b	and wrapped it in linen,
John 19:40b	and wound it in linen clothes
John 19:40b	with the spices, as the manner of the Jews is to bury.
John 19:41a	Now in the place where he was crucified there was a garden;

Matt. 27:60a   And laid it in his own new tomb, which he had hewn out in the rock:

Mark 15:46c   and laid him in a sepulchre which was hewn out of a rock,

Luke 23:53c   and laid it in a sepulchre that was hewn in stone, wherein never man before was laid.

John 19:41a   and in the garden a new sepulchre, wherein was never man yet laid.

Matt. 27:60b   and he rolled a great stone to the door of the sepulchre, and departed.

Mark 15:46d   and rolled a stone unto the door of the sepulchre.

Luke 23:54   And that † was the preparation [day], and the sabbath drew on.

John 19:42   There laid they Jesus therefore because of the Jews' preparation day; for the sepulchre was nigh at hand.

Matt. 27:61a   And there was Mary Magdalene, and the other Mary,

Mark 15:47a   And Mary Magdalene and Mary the mother of Joses

Luke 23:55a   And the women also, which came with him from Galilee, followed after,

Matt. 27:61b   sitting over against the sepulchre.

Mark 15:47b   beheld where he was laid.

Luke 23:55b   and † [beheld] the sepulchre, and [beheld] how his body was laid.

Luke 23:56a   And they returned, and prepared spices and ointments;

Mark 16:1   And when the sabbath was past, Mary Magdalene, and Mary the mother of James, and Salome, had bought sweet spices,

Luke 23:56b   and rested the sabbath day according to the commandment.

Part 7

The Seventh Day of the Week

Saturday

86. Ye Have a Watch

Matt. 27:62–66

Matt. 27:62   Now the next day, that followed the day of the preparation, the chief priests and Pharisees came together unto Pilate,

Matt. 27:63   Saying, Sir, we remember that that deceiver said, while he was yet alive, After three days I will rise again.

Matt. 27:64a   Command therefore that the sepulchre be made sure until the third day, lest his disciples come by night, and steal him away,
Matt. 27:64b   and say unto the people, He is risen from the dead: so the last error shall be worse than the first.

Matt. 27:65   Pilate said unto them, Ye have a watch: go your way, make it as sure as ye can.

Matt. 27:66   So they went, and made the sepulchre sure, sealing the stone, and setting a watch.

PART 8

The Lord's Day

Sunday

87. Who Shall Roll Us Away the Stone?

Matt. 28:1–4; Mark 16:2–4; Luke 24:1–2; John 20:1

Matt. 28:1a	In the end of the sabbath,
Mark 16:1a	And when the sabbath was past,
Mark 16:2a	And very early in the morning as it began to dawn
Luke 24:1a	Now† very early in the morning,
John 20:1a	[early, when it was yet dark,] [at the rising of the sun.]
Matt. 28:1a	toward the first day of the week,
Mark 16:2a	the first day of the week,
Luke 24:1a	[upon the first day of the week,]
John 20:1a	The first day of the week,
Matt. 28:2a	And, behold, there was a great earthquake: for the angel of the Lord descended from heaven, and came and rolled back the stone from the
Matt. 28:2b	door, and sat upon it.
Matt. 28:3	His countenance was like lightening, and his raiment white as snow:
Matt. 28:4	And for fear of him the keepers did shake, and became as dead men.
Matt. 28:1b	came Mary Magdalene and the other Mary
Mark 16:1b	Mary Magdalene, and Mary the mother of James, and Salome
Luke 24:1c	[they]
Luke 24:10a	Mary Magdalene, [and Mary the mother of James], and Joanna,† and certain others
John 20:1b	It was cometh Mary Magdalene† and other women
Mark 16:1c	[sweet spices] had bought†, that they might come and anoint him.
Luke 24:1d	with them.
Luke 24:10b	that were with them, bringing the spices which they had prepared,
Matt. 28:1c	that were to see the sepulchre
Mark 16:2b	they came unto the sepulchre†
Luke 24:1b	they came unto the sepulchre
John 20:1c	unto the sepulchre.
Mark 16:3	And they said among themselves, Who shall roll us away the stone from the door of the sepulchre?

121

Mark 16:4   And when they looked, they saw that the stone was rolled away: for it was very great.

Luke 24:2   And they found the stone rolled away from the sepulchre.

John 20:1d   and seeth the stone taken away from the sepulchre.

88. Then She [Mary] Runneth

John 19:2

John 19:2a   Then she runneth, and cometh to Simon Peter, and to the other disciple, whom Jesus loved, and saith unto them, They have taken away the

John 19:2b   Lord out of the sepulchre, and we know not where they have laid him.

89. He Is Not Here

Matt. 28:5–7; Mark 16:5–7; Luke 24:3–8

Mark 16:5a   And entering into the sepulchre,

Luke 24:3   And they entered in, and found not the body of the Lord Jesus.

Luke 24:4a   And it came to pass, as they were much perplexed thereabout,

Mark 16:5b   they saw a young man sitting on the right side, clothed in a long white garment;

Luke 24:4b   two men stood by them in shining garments

Mark 16:5c   and they were affrighted.

Luke 24:5a   And as they were afraid, and bowed down their faces to the earth,

Matt. 28:5   And the angel answered and said unto the women, Fear not ye: for I know that ye seek Jesus, which was crucified.

Mark 16:6a   And he saith unto them, Be not affrighted: Ye seek Jesus of Nazareth, which was crucified:

Luke 24:5b   they said unto them,

Matt. 28:6   He is not here: for he is risen, as he said. Come, see the place where the Lord lay.

Mark 16:6b   [he is not here:] he is risen; † behold the place where they laid him.

Luke 24:5c   Why seek ye the living among the dead?

Luke 24:6a   He is not here, but is risen:

Matt. 28:7a   And go quickly, and tell his disciples that he is risen from the dead;

Luke 24:6b	remember how he spake unto you when he was yet in Galilee,
Luke 24:7	Saying, The Son of man must be delivered into the hands of sinful men, and be crucified, and the third day rise again.
Matt. 28:7b	and, behold, he goeth before you into Galilee; there shall ye see him:
Mark 16:7	But go your way, tell his disciples and Peter that he goeth before you into Galilee: there shall ye see him, as he said unto you.
Matt. 28:7c	lo, I have told you.
Luke 24:8	And they remembered his words,

90. They Went Out Quickly
Matt. 28:8; Mark 16:8; Luke 24:9-11

Matt. 28:8a	And they departed quickly from the sepulchre with fear and great joy;
Mark 16:8a	And they went out quickly, and fled from the sepulchre; for they trembled and were amazed:
Luke 24:9a	And returned from the sepulchre,
Matt. 28:8b	and did run to bring his disciples word.
Mark 16:8b	neither said they any thing to any man; for they were afraid.
Luke 24:9b	and told all these things unto the eleven, and to all the rest.
Luke 24:10a	It was Mary Magdalene, and Joanna, and Mary the mother of James, and other women that were with them, which told these things unto
Luke 24:10b	the apostles.
Luke 24:11	And their words seemed to them as idle tales, and they believed them not.

91. They Ran Both Together
Luke 24:12; John 20:3–10

John 20:3	Peter therefore went forth, and that other disciple, and came to the sepulchre.
John 20:4	So they ran both together: and the other disciple did outrun Peter, and came first to the sepulchre.
John 20:5	And he stooping down, and looking in, saw the linen clothes lying; yet went he not in.

Luke 24:12a	Then arose Peter, and ran unto the sepulchre; and stooping down, he beheld the linen clothes laid by themselves,
John 20:6	Then cometh Simon Peter following him, and went into the sepulchre, and seeth the linen clothes lie,
John 20:7	And the napkin, that was about his head, not lying with the linen clothes, but wrapped together in a place by itself.
John 20:8	Then went in also that other disciple, which came first to the sepulchre, and he saw, and believed.
John 20:9	For as yet they knew not the scripture, that he must rise again from the dead.
Luke 24:12b	and departed, wondering in himself at that which was come to pass.
John 20:10	Then the disciples went away again unto their own home.

92. Touch Me Not

Mark 16:9–11; John 20:11–18

Mark 16:9	¶ Now when Jesus was risen early the first day of the week, he appeared first to Mary Magdalene, out of whom he had cast seven devils.
John 20:11	¶ But Mary stood without at the sepulchre weeping: and as she wept, she stooped down, and looked into the sepulchre,
John 20:12	And seeth two angels in white sitting, the one at the head, and the other at the feet, where the body of Jesus had lain.
John 20:13a	And they say unto her, Woman, why weepest thou? She saith unto them, Because they have taken away my Lord, and
John 20:13b	I know not where they have laid him.
John 20:14	And when she had thus said, she turned herself back, and saw Jesus standing, and knew not that it was Jesus.
John 20:15a	Jesus saith unto her, Woman, why weepest thou? whom seekest thou? She, supposing him to be the gardener, saith unto him,
John 20:15b	Sir, if thou have borne him hence, tell me where thou hast laid him, and I will take him away.
John 20:16	Jesus saith unto her, Mary. She turned herself, and saith unto him, Rabboni; which is to say, Master.
John 20:17a	Jesus saith unto her, Touch me not; for I am not yet ascended to my Father: but go to my brethren, and say unto them,
John 20:17b	I ascend unto my Father, and your Father; and to my God, and your God.
Mark 16:10	And she went and told them that had been with him, as they mourned and wept.
John 20:18a	Mary Magdalene came and told the disciples that she had seen the Lord,

John 20:18b and that he had spoken these things unto her.

Mark 16:11 And they, when they had heard that he was alive, and had been seen of her, believed not.

93. Be Not Afraid
Matt. 28:9–10

Matt. 28:9 ¶ And as they went to tell his disciples, behold, Jesus met them, saying, All hail. And they came and held him by the feet, and worshipped him.

Matt. 28:10 Then said Jesus unto them, Be not afraid: go tell my brethren that they go into Galilee, and there shall they see me.

94. And the Graves Were Opened
Matt. 27:52–53

Matt. 27:52 And the graves were opened; and many bodies of the saints which slept arose,

Matt. 27:53 And came out of the graves after his resurrection, and went into the holy city, and appeared unto many.

95. We Will Persuade Him and Secure You
Matt. 28:11–15

Matt. 28:11 ¶ Now when they were going, behold, some of the watch came into the city, and shewed unto the chief priests all the things that were done.

Mark 28:12 And when they were assembled with the elders, and had taken counsel, they gave large money unto the soldiers,

Mark 28:13 Saying, Say ye, His disciples came by night, and stole him away while we slept.

Mark 28:14 And if this come to the governor's ears, we will persuade him, and secure you.

Mark 28:15 So they took the money, and did as they were taught: and this saying is commonly reported among the Jews until this day.

96. A Village Called Emmaus
Mark 16:12–13; Luke 24:13–35

Mark 16:12a
Luke 24:a ¶ After that he appeared in another form unto
¶ And, behold,

Mark 16:12b two of them, as they walked, and went into the country.
Luke 24:13b two of them went that same day

Luke 24:13b to a village called Emmaus, which was from Jerusalem about threescore furlongs.

Luke 24:14 And they talked together of all these things which had happened.

Luke 24:15 And it came to pass, that, while they communed together and reasoned, Jesus himself drew near, and went with them.

Luke 24:16 But their eyes were holden that they should not know him.

Luke 24:17 And he said unto them, What manner of communications are these that ye have one to another, as ye walk, and are sad?

Luke 24:18a And the one of them, whose name was Cleopas, answering said unto him, Art thou only a stranger in Jerusalem, and hast not known
Luke 24:18b the things which are come to pass there in these days?

Luke 24:19a And he said unto them, What things? And they said unto him, Concerning Jesus of Nazareth, which was a prophet mighty in deed and word
Luke 24:19b before God and all the people:

Luke 24:20 And how the chief priests and our rulers delivered him to be condemned to death, and have crucified him.

Luke 24:21 But we trusted that it had been he which should have redeemed Israel: and beside all this, to day is the third day since these things were done.

Luke 24:22 Yea, and certain women also of our company made us astonished, which were early at the sepulchre;

Luke 24:23 And when they found not his body, they came, saying, that they had also seen a vision of angels, which said that he was alive.

Luke 24:24 And certain of them which were with us went to the sepulchre, and found it even so as the women had said: but him they saw not.

Luke 24:25 Then he said unto them, O fools, and slow of heart to believe all that the prophets have spoken:

Luke 24:26 Ought not Christ to have suffered these things, and to enter into his glory?

126

Luke 24:27	And beginning at Moses and all the prophets, he expounded unto them in all the scriptures the things concerning himself.
Luke 24:28	And they drew nigh unto the village, whither they went: and he made as though he would have gone further.
Luke 24:29	But they constrained him, saying, Abide with us: for it is toward evening, and the day is far spent. And he went in to tarry with them.
Luke 24:30	And it came to pass, as he sat at meat with them, he took bread, and blessed it, and brake, and gave to them.
Luke 24:31	And their eyes were opened, and they knew him; and he vanished out of their sight.
Luke 24:32	And they said one to another, Did not our heart burn within us, while he talked with us by the way, and while he opened to us the scriptures?
Mark 16:13a **Luke 24:33**	And they went and And they rose up the same hour, and returned to Jerusalem, and found the eleven gathered together, and them that were with them,
Luke 24:34	Saying, The Lord is risen indeed, and hath appeared to Simon.
Mark 16:13b **Luke 24:35**	and told it unto the residue: And they told what things were done in the way, and how he was known of them in breaking of bread.
Mark 16:13c	neither believed they them.

97. The Same Day at Evening
Mark 16:14; Luke 24:35–48; John 20:19–23

Mark 16:14a **Luke 24:36a** **John 20:19a**	Afterward And as they thus spake, Then the same day at evening, being the first day of the week,
John 20:19b	when the doors were shut where the disciples were assembled for fear of the Jews,
Mark 16:14b **John 20:19c** **Luke 24:36b**	he appeared unto the eleven as they sat at meat, came Jesus and stood in the midst, and saith unto them, Peace be unto you. Jesus himself stood in the midst of them, and saith unto them, Peace be unto you.
Luke 24:37	But they were terrified and affrighted, and supposed that they had seen a spirit.

Luke 24:38	And he said unto them, Why are ye troubled? and why do thoughts arise in your hearts?
Luke 24:39	Behold my hands and my feet, that it is I myself: handle me, and see; for a spirit hath not flesh and bones, as ye see me have.
Luke 24:40	And when he had thus spoken, he shewed them his hands and his feet.
John 20:20	And when he had so said, he shewed unto them his hands and his side. Then were the disciples glad, when they saw the Lord.
Luke 24:41	And while they yet believed not for joy, and wondered, he said unto them, Have ye here any meat?
Luke 24:42	And they gave him a piece of a broiled fish, and of an honeycomb.
Luke 24:43	And he took it, and did eat before them.
Luke 24:44a	And he said unto them, These are the words which I spake unto you, while I was yet with you, that all things must be fulfilled,
Luke 24:44b	which were written in the law of Moses, and in the prophets, and in the psalms, concerning me.
Luke 24:45	Then opened he their understanding, that they might understand the scriptures,
Mark 16:14c	and upbraided them with their unbelief and hardness of heart, because they believed not them which had seen him after he was risen.
Luke 24:46	And said unto them, Thus it is written, and thus it behoved Christ to suffer, and to rise from the dead the third day:
Luke 24:47	And that repentance and remission of sins should be preached in his name among all nations, beginning at Jerusalem.
Luke 24:48	And ye are witnesses of these things.
John 20:21	Then said Jesus to them again, Peace be unto you: as my Father hath sent me, even so send I you.
John 20:22	And when he had said this, he breathed on them, and saith unto them, Receive ye the Holy Ghost:
John 20:23	Whose soever sins ye remit, they are remitted unto them; and whose soever sins ye retain, they are retained.

PART 9

Eight Days Later

Sunday

98. My Lord and My God

John 20:24–29

John 20:24 ¶ But Thomas, one of the twelve, called Didymus, was not with them when Jesus came.

John 20:25a
John 20:25b The other disciples therefore said unto him, We have seen the Lord. But he said unto them, Except I shall see in his hands the print of the nails, and put my finger into the print of the nails, and thrust my hand into his side, I will not believe.

John 20:26a
John 20:26b ¶ And after eight days again his disciples were within, and Thomas with them: then came Jesus, the doors being shut, and stood in the midst, and said, Peace be unto you.

John 20:27a
John 20:27b Then saith he to Thomas, Reach hither thy finger, and behold my hands; and reach hither thy hand, and thrust it into my side: and be not faithless, but believing.

John 20:28 And Thomas answered and said unto him, My Lord and my God.

John 20:29a
John 20:29b Jesus saith unto him, Thomas, because thou hast seen me, thou hast believed: blessed are they that have not seen, and yet have believed.

PART 10

Forty Day Ministry

99. I Go a Fishing

John 21:1–14

John 21:1	After these things Jesus shewed himself again to the disciples at the sea of Tiberias; and on this wise shewed he himself.
John 21:2a **John 21:2b**	There were together Simon Peter, and Thomas called Didymus, and Nathanael of Cana in Galilee, and the sons of Zebedee, and two other of his disciples.
John 21:3a **John 21:3b**	Simon Peter saith unto them, I go a fishing. They say unto him, We also go with thee. They went forth, and entered into a ship immediately; and that night they caught nothing.
John 21:4	But when the morning was now come, Jesus stood on the shore: but the disciples knew not that it was Jesus.
John 21:5	Then Jesus saith unto them, Children, have ye any meat? They answered him, No.
John 21:6a **John 21:6b**	And he said unto them, Cast the net on the right side of the ship, and ye shall find. They cast therefore, and now they were not able to draw it for the multitude of fishes.
John 21:7a **John 21:7b**	Therefore that disciple whom Jesus loved saith unto Peter, It is the Lord. Now when Simon Peter heard that it was the Lord, he girt his fisher's coat unto him, (for he was naked,) and did cast himself into the sea.
John 21:8a **John 21:8b**	And the other disciples came in a little ship; (for they were not far from land, but as it were two hundred cubits,) dragging the net with fishes.
John 21:9	As soon then as they were come to land, they saw a fire of coals there, and fish laid thereon, and bread.
John 21:10	Jesus saith unto them, Bring of the fish which ye have now caught.
John 21:11a **John 21:11b**	Simon Peter went up, and drew the net to land full of great fishes, an hundred and fifty and three: and for all there were so many, yet was not the net broken.
John 21:12	Jesus saith unto them, Come and dine. And none of the disciples durst ask him, Who art thou? knowing that it was the Lord.
John 21:13	Jesus then cometh, and taketh bread, and giveth them, and fish likewise.
John 21:14	This is now the third time that Jesus shewed himself to his disciples, after that he was risen from the dead.

100. Lovest Thou Me More Than These?

John 21:15–17

John 21:15a ¶ So when they had dined, Jesus saith to Simon Peter, Simon, son of Jonas, lovest thou me more than these? He saith unto him, Yea, Lord;
John 21:15b thou knowest that I love thee. He saith unto him, Feed my lambs.

John 21:16a He saith to him again the second time, Simon, son of Jonas, lovest thou me? He saith unto him, Yea, Lord; thou knowest that I love thee.
John 21:16b He saith unto him, Feed my sheep.

John 21:17a He saith unto him the third time, Simon, son of Jonas, lovest thou me? Peter was grieved because he said unto him the third time, Lovest thou me?
John 21:17b And he said unto him, Lord, thou knowest all things; thou knowest that I love thee. Jesus saith unto him, Feed my sheep.

101. Follow Me

John 21:18–19

John 21:18a Verily, verily, I say unto thee, When thou wast young, thou girdedst thyself, and walkedst whither thou wouldest: but when thou shalt be old,
John 21:18b thou shalt stretch forth thy hands, and another shall gird thee, and carry thee whither thou wouldest not.

John 21:19 This spake he, signifying by what death he should glorify God. And when he had spoken this, he saith unto him, Follow me.

102. What Shall This Man Do?

John 21:20–23

John 21:20a Then Peter, turning about, seeth the disciple whom Jesus loved following; which also leaned on his breast at supper, and said, Lord,
John 21:20b which is he that betrayeth thee?

John 21:21 Peter seeing him saith to Jesus, Lord, and what shall this man do?

John 21:22 Jesus saith unto him, If I will that he tarry till I come, what is that to thee? follow thou me.

John 21:23a Then went this saying abroad among the brethren, that that disciple should not die: yet Jesus said not unto him, He shall not die; but,
John 21:23b If I will that he tarry till I come, what is that to thee?

103. Go Ye into All the World

Matthew 28:16–20; Mark 16:15–18

Matt. 28:16 ¶ Then the eleven disciples went away into Galilee, into a mountain where Jesus had appointed them.

Matt. 28: 17 And when they saw him, they worshipped him: but some doubted.

Matt. 28:18
Mark 16:15a And Jesus came and spake unto them, saying, All power is given unto me in heaven and in earth.
And he said unto them,

Matt. 28:19a ¶ Go ye therefore, and teach all nations,
Mark 16:15b Go ye into all the world, and preach the gospel to every creature.

Matt. 28:19b baptizing them in the name of the Father, and of the Son, and of the Holy Ghost:

Matt. 28:20a Teaching them to observe all things whatsoever I have commanded you:

Mark 16:16 He that believeth and is baptized shall be saved; but he that believeth not shall be damned.

Mark 16:17 And these signs shall follow them that believe; In my name shall they cast out devils; they shall speak with new tongues;

Mark 16:18 They shall take up serpents; and if they drink any deadly thing, it shall not hurt them; they shall lay hands on the sick, and they shall recover.

Matt. 28:20b and lo, I am with you alway, even unto the end of the world. Amen.

104. He Was Parted from Them

Luke 24:49–53

Luke 24:49 ¶ And, behold, I send the promise of my Father upon you: but tarry ye in the city of Jerusalem, until ye be endued with power from on high.

Luke 24:50 ¶ And he led them out as far as to Bethany, and he lifted up his hands, and blessed them.

Luke 24:51 And it came to pass, while he blessed them, he was parted from them, and carried up into heaven.

Luke 24:52 And they worshipped him, and returned to Jerusalem with great joy:

Luke 24:53 And were continually in the temple, praising and blessing God. Amen.

137

105. That Ye Might Believe That Jesus Is the Christ
John 20:30–31; John 21:24–25

John 20:30 ¶ And many other signs truly did Jesus in the presence of his disciples, which are not written in this book:

John 20:31 But these are written, that ye might believe that Jesus is the Christ, the Son of God; and that believing ye might have life through his name.

John 21:24 This is the disciple which testifieth of these things, and wrote these things: and we know that his testimony is true.

John 21:25a
John 21:25b And there are also many other things which Jesus did, the which, if they should be written every one, I suppose that even the world itself could not contain the books that should be written. Amen.

www.ingramcontent.com/pod-product-compliance
Lightning Source LLC
Chambersburg PA
CBHW081213020426
42331CB00012B/3015